Not every day does a book come along that is simultaneously for the church and for the secular world, but Dan Scott's book is precisely that. Brilliantly and compassionately written, he provides an introduction to areas of thought that most of us know too little about. You will want to give this to your Christian and non-Christian friends. It is urgently needed, full of knowledge, doctrinally sound, and deeply appreciated by me.

DR. R.T. KENDALL
Former minister of Westminster Chapel, London, England

I am enjoying this book on world religions. It is not only accurate, clear, and irenic but also firmly evangelical. It is entrancing to read, and I find it hard to put down. The students who are assigned to read it will find it easy to do their duty and find themselves well informed and clothed in the love and humility that commends the gospel.

RIGHT REVEREND JOHN H. RODGERS JR. THD
Bishop in the Anglican Mission in America
Interim Dean and President of Trinity School for Ministry

faith
to faith

DAN SCOTT

HARVEST HOUSE PUBLISHERS

EUGENE, OREGON

Cover by Left Coast Design, Portland, Oregon

Cover photo © Milena Boniek / PhotoAlto / Getty Images

Dan Scott: This Work published in association with the Conversant Media Group, P.O. Box 3006, Redmond, WA 98007.

ConversantLife.com is a trademark of Conversant Media Group. Harvest House Publishers, Inc., is a licensee of the trademark ConversantLife.com.

FAITH TO FAITH
Copyright © 2008 by Dan Scott
Published by Harvest House Publishers
Eugene, Oregon 97402
www.harvesthousepublishers.com

Library of Congress Cataloging-in-Publication Data
Scott, Dan, 1953-
Faith to faith / Dan Scott.
    p. cm.
ISBN-13: 978-0-7369-2350-7
ISBN-10: 0-7369-2350-0
1. Christianity and other religions. I. Title.
BR127.S36 2008
261.2—dc22
                                        2007052794

To Pastor Eric Falk and Emmy Scott

I'll meet you at the wrap-up, just inside the Eastern Gate.

Acknowledgments

A number of people made important contributions to the research and editing of this book. Leah and Thomas Payne of Vanderbilt Divinity School gave invaluable advice about several chapters. Liz Patrick worked untold hours with edits and rewrites. Vickie Riley, Denise Palma, and Rev. Allan Ellis read the manuscript in early stages and gave important feedback to strengthen its biblical and literary qualities. Terry Glaspey and Gene Skinner, my editors at Harvest House, walked through the entire process with me. The people at Conversantlife.com, particularly Peter Schumerth, were encouraging. And finally, thanks to the people of Christ Church, whose support and love is an enduring joy.

contents

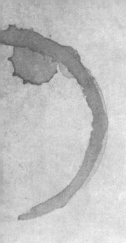

what is
a seeker?

The first time I saw her, she was standing by the vending machine outside our classroom. As I got closer, I noticed she smelled of sandalwood and rose. She had a string of beads woven in her hair. Around her neck was a thin rope on which hung a picture of a brown man sitting in a half-lotus position. Glancing at the picture, I saw a splash of color on the man's forehead. His hand was raised in blessing, and I wondered who he was praying for and why.

When I realized that I was staring at the picture, I forced myself to look into her eyes. I needed to find out why she had asked to speak to me after class.

"What did you think of the lecture?" she asked.

"Well," I replied with some caution, "the professor was certainly interesting. He convinced me that I need to know more about Bowley and attachment theory."

She nodded. She obviously did not want to talk about psychology.

What does *she want?* I wondered as I played with the wedding band on my finger.

"Someone told me that you are a Christian minister," she said.

"Well, yes, I am," now taking on my more professional pastor's voice.

"Would you mind talking with me a moment about a spiritual question?" she asked.

Now I noticed that she too was nervous. "Of course," I said. "Where do we begin?"

"Well, I had a dream...first though, you need to know that I've been sick; otherwise you can't make sense of my dream. Anyway, in this dream I'm standing on a bridge in a beautiful park, worrying about my illness. As I am standing on the bridge, the Christ suddenly walks out of the shadows and onto the bridge. Then He begins talking to me—don't you think it's strange that the Christ would come to a Hindu?" she suddenly interjected.

"Not at all," I said. "That sounds like Jesus. But what happened next?"

"Well, He kept speaking to me very kindly, like you would expect from an enlightened spiritual master. He told me that if I would give Him my sickness, He would heal me. When I replied that I didn't know how to give Him my sickness, He just reached His hands into my body and pulled out a foul-smelling glob of nasty stuff, and it dissolved in His hands."

She paused for my reaction.

"Wow. That's interesting," I said. "Is that all?" (I knew there was more to the story because she had become uncomfortable.)

"No, there's more. I just don't want to offend you."

Too intrigued to let her stop there, I encouraged her to go on.

She played with the strand of beads in her hair as she continued. "Christ ripped off a piece of His skin," she said. "As He handed it to me, He said, 'Eat this; it will make you well.' Those words moved me. I have thought about them for weeks now. What do they mean?"

I didn't know when my eyes had become moist. I only knew that this was a holy moment, not only for her but for me as well. We—this Hindu woman and I—were now in God's presence together. What did it mean? What was I to do with it?

I whispered a response. "You have seen Jesus. That's the way He talks."

Emboldened by my response, she leaned forward as though she were about to make an unreasonable request. "Would you mind if I visit your church sometime?" she asked. "I need to learn more about Jesus."

That was the day I met a real seeker.

For years I had been listening to American Christians debate about how to reach "seekers." I had never considered that we should define the term before debating it. I realized that day with the Hindu lady that we have been defining "seeker" as someone who struggles being in the same room with a cross, hearing a hymn, or tolerating prayer that becomes emotional or reverent. Now I had met a real seeker, a woman who wanted to talk about the intimate parts of my faith even though she practiced another religion. I realized that in this new global culture, we Christians need missionary skills more than marketing techniques.

This Hindu woman had a need. She wanted to meet God. She wanted to learn about my faith. She was not asking me to hide my beliefs, to put away the symbols of my religion, or to mold my spirituality to accommodate her. She just wanted to talk.

Since that encounter, I have discovered that our country is full of such seekers. These people are not terrified of reverence and spirituality; on the contrary, they are famished for spiritual experience. Nonetheless, few of these seekers come to Christian churches now. As it turns out, we have been too busy eliminating spirituality from our worship and doctrine from our teaching. Therefore, when they do come to church, they often struggle to find the purpose for the gathering.

As a Pentecostal child, I learned about the gift of tongues. I did not learn much about the "gift of ears." As a result, I had become less comfortable relating to non-Christians who seek after God than to secular folks who do not. Somehow, I had to shake off the secular trance that mesmerizes much of American evangelicalism. To do that, I needed to rediscover the roots of my own faith, needed to relearn the spiritual language of those who had walked with God through the centuries. I also needed to learn how to listen, with respect and with genuine curiosity, to the questions and beliefs of the world's spiritual seekers. Perhaps then I would have something to say.

After that encounter with the Hindu lady, I began thinking—if Jesus wants to visit people who don't know Him, maybe I should follow His example. That's what I have tried to do since.

I have remained an orthodox, evangelical Christian. In fact, my faith in Christ and His church has deepened. However, I also have discovered that I have nothing to lose from showing kindness and respect toward people of other religions. I have found out that Christ is still compelling, even to people who are not impressed with His church. I discovered that when people meet Jesus through the words, actions, and demeanor of His followers, they love Him. How could they not?

Mostly, my shift in attitude was a private experience for some time. I really actually didn't know many people who practiced other religions.

My attitude toward other religions was put to the test in the fall of 2002. I was living in Phoenix at the time, pastoring a church and working part-time on the staff of a mental health clinic. Both of these roles had pushed me to become acquainted with the leaders of other Christian groups in Arizona. I had become increasingly active on municipal and state committees, organizing assistance for the poor, the disabled, and the uneducated. As a conservative evangelical minister, I was often at odds with the theology and political ideology of other clergypersons in these groups. Nonetheless, we usually were able to move past our differences to organize food distribution, health care, and other social services that our various constituencies required.

In one of these groups I met Glen McKee, the controversial head of the Arizona Ecumenical Council. We had known one another for five years when he asked me to participate in his upcoming Interfaith Conference. He wanted me to present the history and practice of Protestant Christianity. Glen assured me that I would have full freedom to present the faith as I believed it.

"Well, Glen, that all sounds good," I replied. "Just remember that I am an evangelical, committed to orthodox Christianity. Also don't forget that I have a Pentecostal background. That means that many Protestants, on both the right and the left, do not view me as a typical Protestant."

"Yeah, I know," he responded, "but you're honest. I know you'll represent Protestantism as broadly and fairly as you can."

"Well, in that case, I'll do my best," I said.

A few days later, I received a packet of materials from Glen's office. I discovered that the three-day conference would be held at the Franciscan retreat center. Representatives of the major world religions would each have an hour to present a brief overview of their faiths. We would then open the floor for questions and discussion from the attendees. All of the presenters would eat together between sessions. We were also expected to participate in a common worship service at the conclusion of the conference.

Hmmm…that presented a problem. I called Glen.

"I can't participate in your interfaith conference," I said. "I would enjoy hearing the various presentations and participating in the discussions. I would certainly learn a lot. I am more than willing to eat together with the others. However, I will not join the representatives of other religions for an interfaith worship service."

There was silence on the other end of the line. Finally, when I heard Glen's gentle voice, his tone told me that I had hurt him.

"I'm shocked, Dan," he replied. "You have always been so kind to everyone in our meetings. You have just received an award from the city for promoting racial unity. Why this sudden change of heart?"

"Glen," I replied, "friendship is one thing; sharing different viewpoints is vital in our dangerous and changing world. However, worship is an expression of our spiritual intimacy with God and with other believers. I can eat with a Buddhist and have wonderful conversation with him. We may even become good friends, but how can we pray together? A Buddhist doesn't believe anyone is up there to talk to! What a Christian calls worship and what a Buddhist calls a meditation are not the same thing at all! I would think that a common worship service would present a problem for a Buddhist as well.

"I use the Buddhists as an example," I continued, "because they are actually less problematic for me than someone from, say, the Wicca community. Buddhists are philosophers. The practitioners of Wicca, at least as I understand them, encourage us to entertain what Christians believe to be evil spirits. The Scriptures forbid me to have any sort of spiritual connection with people who practice such things."

"Wow. This is disappointing," he said. "Are they not the people of God as much as you?"

"In a sense, they are," I hastened to add. "They are all made in God's image and likeness. Christ died for them all. He loves them all. I certainly should treat them kindly and respectfully. I will not, however, pray with them. I can pray *for* them, but not with them."

In the end, the Ecumenical Council and the Interfaith Commission of Arizona decided not to withdraw their invitation. I would still represent Protestant Christianity. I would participate in every facet of the conference except for the interfaith worship service.

This book is a fictionalized account of that three-day conference. I have changed all the names and reconstructed the various presentations, however. My aim was not to give you a historically accurate picture of that conference but rather to give my fellow Christians as accurate a picture as possible of the beliefs and practices of the various world religions. Many of our neighbors and family members now belong to these faiths, and we need to know how to relate to them.

This book is too small (and my topic too broad) to adequately represent any particular faith. To gain deeper knowledge of a specific faith, a reader must find material more narrowly focused on that religion. Also, a follower of any of the religions represented in this book will probably be disappointed with the way I have presented it. Every religion is a world of its own, filled with seemingly infinite layers of beliefs and practice. The outsider necessarily experiences a religion that is not his own in a woefully incomplete and superficial way. This reality will be evident in this book.

That said, I believe we need a book like this. Buddhists, Hindus, and Taoists were once a world away. Years ago, missionaries showed us slides of their distant temples, filled with colorfully dressed worshippers who seemed so different from us. Now, the Taoist may be our cousin whom we see at Thanksgiving; the Buddhist can be a social worker we meet on a city planning committee. We don't have the luxury of not knowing how these friends and fellow citizens form their thoughts and frame their opinions.

We must know about the great religions for another reason: Many of our neighbors find them enticing. They find them attractive because they seem to offer something that many seekers believe they will not find in a Christian church—answers about meaning and purpose to life, a community that transcends time and space, and the transformation of self. It is hurtful to hear this, but it is true. To the outsider, American forms of faith often seem to be corporately sound and politically active but spiritually detached. So we need to know how to meet the real seekers of the earth and to become bridges on which the risen Christ may meet them and heal their soul's diseases. In so doing, we may well find meaning for our own lives and healing for our own souls.

oh my, **other people**
are **out there!**

Driving across Phoenix on my way to the interfaith conference, I was thankful that our city government had finally started installing left turn signals. For years, some guy in the traffic engineer's office (whom I had once uncharitably called "the caveman") had decided that Phoenix did not need left turn signals! People drove to the center of the intersection, waited for their light to turn red, and then turned left as fast as they could. They rushed to get to where they wanted to go before the other stream of traffic arrived to the space they had just occupied. This terrifying game had killed a lot of people before the caveman finally retired. Now the city had installed hundreds of left turn signals. Life had become a little safer for drivers like me, people who ponder and reflect as they move about town.

I needed some time to ponder! I was getting a little worried about this conference. *Who will see me there?* I wondered. I had politely refused to join the Ecumenical Council for years despite being invited to do so a number of times. I was willing to work with the council on public projects, but I seriously disagreed with most of its members, both theologically and politically. Some of the members of the council were my friends nonetheless. To some people, that made me spiritually suspect. One radio talk show host had recently denounced me on his show because of my personal friendship with Phoenix's Roman Catholic bishop. The buzz had made some of the people in my church anxious, and speculations had been flying like wild through the Internet. Our church sure didn't need any more of that.

As I passed Roberto's Taco Shop on Seventh Street, I began reviewing my spiritual journey. I remembered the time I had been frightened to receive Communion in a Baptist church. I thought about how Father Thomas, a priest who worked with impoverished people in Juarez, had once asked my forgiveness for having been reluctant to pray with me (heretic that I was!). I recalled my visit with Patriarch Ilyia of the Georgian Orthodox church in the days after Gorbachev had ordered the government to reopen the Georgian churches. I thought about how I had danced with Pentecostal believers in the Philippines.

Life had certainly taken me places and connected me to people that would have surprised me as a younger man. However, almost all of these experiences had been with Christians of some sort. Whether I had agreed with them or not, we had at least been able to refer to a common sacred text and to a common set of beliefs.

This would be different. The people I was about to meet would have sacred texts of their own. Their rituals and beliefs would seem as foreign to me as my faith was to them. How would we even talk to one another about spiritual things with civility while remaining true to our deepest convictions?

I was supposed to tell them about Protestantism, so I had prepared a historical overview of the subject. *But what is Protestantism, anyway?* I wondered

Once upon a time, Protestants confessed a set of core beliefs—the centrality of the Bible, justification by faith, the priesthood of believers, and so forth. Now it seems that "Protestant" means merely "non-Roman-Catholic Western Christian." That is a terribly broad category.

Was I a Protestant? By whose definition?

What did "Protestantism" even mean in today's world?

The people on the Ecumenical Council were not Roman Catholic. They represented groups with roots back to the Reformation, but were they really Protestant? Their view of the Bible was certainly different from those of the Reformers. They were not sure of the physical resurrection of Jesus. They thought that other religions were alternate roads to God. I didn't agree with any of those things. How could both they and I be Protestant?

Driving past the Chinese cultural center on Forty-fourth Street, I marveled at the acres of Asian buildings, just two blocks away from the Serbian

Orthodox church. Then I thought about how the area where both of these places were located was predominantly Hispanic!

That made me think about the church I pastored and all the unrest there, most of it related to race and culture. The older people who had led the church since it was founded were mostly from the American midwest. They seemed to just now be noticing the dramatic social changes that had been going on in our country for most of my life. They were, for example, increasingly angry to hear Spanish being spoken in the hallways of our church. Our Native American members were pressing for more sensitivity to their culture. The young adults wanted to sing Hillsong music with guitars, and the young parents felt that we were not moving fast enough to modernize our children's classroom décor. Meanwhile, our older leaders were feeling as if they were drowning in diversity and special interests.

I didn't have the heart to tell them that we were just now cracking the door of our church, that what they were experiencing was not the full picture but merely a peek at how our city and nation had been changing. I wanted to ask them why, if they were so resistant to diverse cultures, they had not moved their church 30 miles out on the edge of town, where most of them now lived.

Whatever the church leaders had or had not done, I felt increasingly squeezed between the different factions of our church. The church leaders were reluctant to address cultural changes that had become a part of our national identity. Our younger people (and our new converts) looked at life and expressed themselves in ways that our older members simply could not understand. Things had gotten tense.

If our church members find out I'm attending an interfaith conference, they'll throw me out as a heretic, I thought.

Just as I thought this, I saw a bumper sticker on the old truck right in front of me. It said (in Spanish), "If you don't like our country then get the —— out!" Clearly the driver was a Spanish-speaking American, upset about the bombing of the World Trade Center.

At first I just laughed. The driver's ancestors probably lived in Arizona several centuries before the pioneers from the eastern states even arrived on the continent. Arizona was once the northern region of Spain's American empire. When the Americans took over in the years after the Civil War, they inherited this area's Spanish-speaking cities and villages. Nonetheless, Anglos still seemed amazed to hear Spanish in this area. *It makes you wonder what kind of history classes these people attended,* I thought.

As I got closer to the old truck, I could hear the music of northern Mexico wailing out into the street—and into my ears!

I had to admit that even though I speak the language, the music felt like an assault. I noticed that the song was about some poor guy who could not live without the attention of a young señorita named Lucia. The music sounded pitiful; apparently it required beer to be fully appreciated!

I noticed the day before that the Church of Higher Realization on Central Avenue had put up a new sign. Some swami in long flowing robes was smiling at passersby from that sign. Under the swami was the topic for the following Sunday: "How to Connect to Your Higher Self."

My higher self wants away from this loud music, I fumed. *We didn't have to deal with all this stuff when I was a boy in West Virginia!*

We all had been good old-fashioned Christian Americans! Oh, we had a Chinese restaurant. An Orthodox church was downtown—some people whose grandparents were from Lebanon and Syria went there. A few snake handlers met in the mountains near our city. (Okay, more than just a few!) Other than that, the great divisions in our town were between the 19 different kinds of Baptists, the Church of Christ, and the Pentecostals. The Republicans and Democrats didn't exactly see eye to eye, of course. African-Americans lived in a different part of town in our segregated era. The coal miners got in fights sometimes with the absentee landlords who owned the mines. An Italian guy had a steak house. Two Greeks ran a bookstore. Jewish people owned some of the clothing stores downtown. So in retrospect, I suppose we had some diversity. It just didn't seem, well, so diverse back then!

Perhaps it was because English-speaking white people were in a clear majority back then. Maybe that's what made us feel more secure than some people do now. Whatever it was, things have changed.

And the diversity is not just "out there." Much has changed even within the Christian church.

Philip Jenkins claims that Christians in the world's southern hemisphere now outnumber the ones north of the equator. This means that Europeans and North Americans no longer lead the Christian churches. Jenkins believes that Christianity is splitting into two main factions, just as it did in 1054. Back then the church split between the East and West; this time, he believes, the split is occurring between the global south and the global north. In what we used to call the third world, Christianity has been experiencing explosive growth. This demographic is now affecting most Christians in most denominations, whether they think of themselves as on the right or the left.

In the southern hemisphere, Baptists often speak in tongues, Presbyterians have visions, and Methodists cast out demons. In the global south almost every sort of Christian, whether Roman Catholic, Presbyterian, or Pentecostal, tends to believe that Jesus rose physically from the dead and that angels may appear to believers just as they did in Bible times. We might call that "conservatism" except for the fact that in the northern hemisphere, supernatural phenomena tends to upset conservative Christians as much as it does liberal ones.

Liberals usually assert that people in Bible times didn't actually see angels; New Testament accounts of such things were based on hearsay and poetic license. A liberal will certainly insist that no one is going to see an angel today. American conservatives furiously resent this liberal disbelief, at least as it relates to the Bible. However, conservatives generally agree with liberals that such things will not happen today. Christians in the global south however, usually have a difficult time discerning the difference between those positions. They figure that either miracles happened in the Bible or they did not, but if they once did, they probably still do.

So does that make the Christians of the global south conservatives?

Well, the terms we invented to describe our own cultural and political issues don't work with the new believers. Christians in the global south are concerned that so many of their people live in oppressive poverty while a few folk with private airplanes and large plantations keep making rules to keep things the way they have always been. So while they are biblical literalists like their conservative counterparts in North America, they also pray against poverty, hunger, and political oppression. In other words, terms like "liberal" and "conservative" just don't mean very much down there.

Now that the Christians from the global south are moving here, what does that do to our national church culture? The tension between the global south and global north is already splitting the Episcopal Church, USA. That church was well on its way to liberal nirvana until the Nigerians, Rwandans, and Chinese showed up and blew a very loud whistle in the bishops' ears. Then there are the poor Southern Baptists; they felt forced to send out a decree forbidding their missionaries to speak in tongues. Recently one American Pentecostal group went into convulsions because their Ethiopian contingency reopened an old third-century controversy about the dual nature of Christ. (Ethiopians and Egyptians were the ones who opened up that same controversy seventeen hundred years ago!)

The third-world Christians are not keeping their influence south of the equator, as it turns out.

According to one story, a delegation of African Christian leaders who were living in England went to the Archbishop of Canterbury to ask him if they could use his cathedral. This seemed logical to them. He obviously no longer needs his building to accommodate the small crowds that show up to his church. However, the Africans have thousands of people meeting in an old warehouse near the cathedral. The Christian thing to do, the African believers thought, was simply to give them the church.

The Africans seemed genuinely amazed at the Anglican outrage.

What's going on?

Whatever it is, one thing's for sure: The world has changed. People in our cities, in our countries, and inside our churches now see the world very differently from the way people like me see it. We'd be smart to know who they are and how they think.

As I got closer to the Franciscan retreat center, my mind returned to the issue at hand: I was about to meet with people from other religions. How did I feel about them?

One Christian view is that a believer should have nothing to do with people of other faiths. In that view, people of other religions are lost and deceived. Their religions are demonic systems of thought and behavior; the further one stays away from them, the better.

On the other hand, people like Dr. Amos Yong take a different approach. He teaches systematic theology at the conservative Regent University. Yong has been raising eyebrows among a lot of people for his views on the Holy Spirit. He teaches that the Spirit's central work is to prepare people's hearts to receive Christ—a belief that is certainly Orthodox. However, Yong says that Christians are called to discover what the Holy Spirit is doing within the world's religious communities to woo their people toward Christ.[1]

Henry Blackaby, a Southern Baptist, also says things like that. He says that a Christian's job is to discover what God is doing and then join God in doing that work. So how can I find out what God is already doing among the world's peoples? How can I start working with Him instead of retreating into fear and hostility?

I am an orthodox Christian. I do not believe that all paths lead to God.

However, I do believe that God is at work among those who seek Him. Cornelius sought God when he was a pagan. Melchizedek, whoever he was, prayed for Abraham; and Melchizedek wasn't a Hebrew! For that matter, Moses' own father-in-law was a priest, but not a Hebrew one. Things are just not as black-and-white as some Christians would have us to believe about how we should interact with other religions.

Conservatives often cite how the godly kings of Judah destroyed the altars of the idols. However, they usually fail to acknowledge how Daniel became the head of all the magicians and soothsayers in Babylon.

I wonder how that worked? I ask myself. Then a thought runs through my head: *Arizona has ruined me!*

I have tried to learn how to work with this spiritual but non-Christian culture. Phoenix's spiritual vibe is Native-American-shamanistic-pragmatic-motivational-libertarian. Everyone here seems to make up his or her own religion.

A town north of here, Sedona, has to be one of the world's most beautiful places. A lot of people—a whole lot of people—think it's much more than that. Thousands flock there every day to experience the "convergence of cosmic lines of energy." According to them, this energy accumulates in Sedona like few places in the world, at points they call "vortexes." People lay naked on rocks to soak up the energy. (I wanted to see that for myself, but my wife was suspicious that I just wanted to see naked people on rocks!) Fortunately, one vortex is at the Sedona airport, where being naked is against the law. So I went there. I got very still and enjoyed the view. However, I couldn't locate the energy vortex.

My friends laugh at this stuff. I don't. Millions of people take it very seriously. So what is that if not a religion? If a person is willing to travel from Boston to Sedona and lay naked on a rock for a few hours, he has just made a pilgrimage. If he does it again, he must be convinced that he has located a source of supernatural grace.

Some of the people in my church won't even go to Sedona. They say that it has demonic spirits. They don't like Santa Fe, New Mexico either. Same problem—demons! Well, something must be wrong with me because I love both Sedona and Santa Fe. I don't feel the power of the vortex and I don't sense demons. I just think of them as beautiful places.

As I pulled into the Franciscan retreat center, I thought about St. Paul at Mars Hill. I'm no St. Paul; however, it did help me to think about how he must have felt as he climbed Mars Hill to discuss different points of view about God. After I parked the car, I centered myself the way I learned to do long ago: by opening the Scriptures and meditating on the words.

> This God, whom you worship without knowing, is the one I'm telling you about…Since he is Lord of heaven and earth, he doesn't live in man-made temples…He himself gives life and breath to everything, and he satisfies every need. From one man he created all the nations throughout the whole earth…His purpose was for the nations to seek after God and perhaps feel their way toward him and find him—though he is not far from any one of us. For in him we live and move and exist…We are his offspring (Acts 17:23-29 NLT).

Before I got out of the car, I thought once more about the traffic engineer who hated left turn signals. That engineer wasn't trying to kill anyone; he just wanted to keep his town the way he had grown to love it. He liked the Phoenix of his childhood, the way things used to be. He was grieving the changes time had brought to his hometown. The city had grown; it required a more complicated system of traffic management. But the engineer insisted that we keep trying to turn left without a turn signal, gunning our accelerators and endangering our lives so we could maintain his childhood environment. In the end, he lost the Phoenix he knew anyway. Meanwhile, people lost their lives because he wouldn't listen.

So we have to listen. That's often difficult for us.

As I walked toward the retreat center, I thought about how St. Peter reluctantly entered the house of some Italians who had been seeking God. Peter had a vision. He should have been prepared for his encounter, but he didn't fully understand what the vision meant. The implications of the vision were still too scary. He was frightened. We know this because of what Peter blurted out to his astonished hosts when he entered their house. It might sound like this today: "I see that God doesn't care who He hangs out with!"[2]

Nonetheless, Peter found the necessary grace to tell the story of Jesus. When he did, the Holy Spirit did what only He can do; He overshadowed the group with His presence and power.

Oh, that this would happen again, I thought as I walked into the center. However, if the Spirit is going to change people's lives and confirm His Word with such signs, we have to be willing to show up at those places where seekers gather to pray.

I walked into the building more calm and confident than I had been that God loves everyone and that He is the one who is in charge of saving seekers.

My job was just to show up.

the great harmony:
taoism and the chinese worldview

*Live your life in such a way that you will give
out a fragrance for a thousand generations.*

James Redman was a handsome man, about six feet tall. His long black hair (which he wore in a short ponytail) was generously speckled with white and gray. He carried himself like a man accustomed to hard work and equally at ease with any class of people. His clothes were not particularly fashionable, but he wasn't dowdy either. His rust colored, short-sleeve shirt was made of cotton, and he wore jeans and Skechers.

He had a kind face with a subdued but genuine smile.

Glen told us in the introduction that James lived in Eugene, Oregon, where he runs a natural-health center. He is married and has two children—one of them a boy named Tiananmen! His children were not with him, but I assumed the woman sitting under the window to his right must be his wife. I would later discover that my intuition was correct. Her name, she would tell me later, was Bridget.

When I realized that Taoism would be the first religion presented, I saw the logic in the choice. It is one of the world's oldest religions and one of the least threatening to people of other faiths. However, Taoism is the essence of Chinese culture.

Shouldn't a Chinese person be making this presentation? I wondered. I was disappointed, to tell the truth. I wanted to see an ancient Chinese guy with long strands of hair hanging from his chin.

James looked us over. Then he took a deep breath and said with a grin,

Okay, I'm not Chinese.

Wow, can Taoists read minds? I wondered.

If I were you, I would want to hear about Taoism from a Chinese master. Unfortunately, I am as American as they come. I was born in Hot Springs, Arkansas, and was raised Methodist. I listen to James Taylor as often as I can. So telling you how I became attracted to Chinese philosophy and medicine may be the easiest way to tell you what Taoism is about.

I will do my best to explain Taoism, though I have never really identified myself with any specific religious label. I am, therefore, somewhat uneasy with even claiming to be a Taoist. I would prefer to call myself a student of Chinese culture and philosophy.

The best-known text of Taoism, what we call the Tao Te Ching, begins by claiming that those who know the Tao do not name it, and those who name it do not know it. So there you have it—if I tell you what Tao is, I will be revealing that I don't really understand it. However, if I do know what it is, I should confess to you that I cannot explain it to you!

If what I just said makes you want to scream, you are getting close to the heart of Tao!

The Tao—which is, by the way, pronounced with a *d*—is the great unity or underlying pattern from which all individual things emerge. Although the Tao is unknowable, we can experience it. As we do, we learn to live effortlessly. By flowing with the natural direction of the universe—the Tao—we begin living in harmony with all that is.

Hmm…I was not off to a good start! I had decided to take notes, but this was all I had written so far: "If I know what Tao is, I cannot tell you. If I tell you what it is, I don't really understand it." Beside my words, I had drawn an elongated face, its mouth open, gaping in a great silent scream. Under the face I had written, "Are they all crazy?" Then I felt guilty for writing that because Bridget, James's wife, was smiling at me.

No doubt the silent scream in my notebook was showing on my face— I've never been good at hiding my feelings.

I made an effort to look up at James with the studious and admiring gaze of someone who has respect for what he is hearing.

When I was studying at the University of Tennessee in Knoxville, the cold war was in full swing. Many of my friends had decided to study Russian. They said it was to protest against American imperialism. I think they just wanted to shock their parents.

Anyway, Nixon had just gone to China. As I watched the television coverage, I became fascinated by what seemed to me the utterly alien culture of the Chinese people. I also saw a television special about a Chinese man who had his appendix removed without anesthesia—the doctors used acupuncture—and I was seriously intrigued. I wanted to know more.

When I told my parents I had decided to take a Chinese language class, they asked me if I was becoming a Communist. Actually, I was completely apolitical. I told my dad that I wanted to find the meaning of life, to which I remember him replying, "Good luck with that!" My parents thought that learning Chinese would be a total waste of my time. They told me later that they figured that I wouldn't last long with Chinese anyway.

As a matter of fact, I did well in Chinese studies; I ended up taking it for three years. I even tried to get into an exchange program so I could actually study in China. I didn't make the cut, though; I would get the opportunity to do that later. I did meet an interesting person while I was taking Chinese, and he completely changed my life. His name was Dr. Park, and though he was actually from Korea, he had studied Chinese for many years. He taught the language for a couple of semesters while I was at UT, and we became friends.

Dr. Park introduced me to the world of ancient China. He loaned me a number of books to read and discuss with him, among which was the Tao Te Ching and the I Ching. These books became enormously influential in my life—but more on that later.

When we think of China, we must realize that it is unlike any other nation. For one thing, it is the world's oldest continuous civilization. It is larger than Western Europe and, like Europe, is home to many ethnic groups who speak many different languages. What we call Chinese is actually a family of languages. The Chinese dialects are often as mutually incomprehensible to their speakers as French and Italian are to those who speak those languages. Despite these differences, the Chinese people are united by three things:

- a common civilization stretching back through time,

- a common written language that the Chinese, regardless of their particular dialect, understand, and

- a common worldview that unites the Chinese, regardless of their religious affiliation.

Imagine a culture that began about the same time Hammurabi was ruling Babylon but that still exists today. Think about how amazing it is that the Chinese people can still read the words of their distant ancestors with complete comprehension. It would be as if the European people, despite their different languages, were able to read the original words of Homer, St. Paul, Virgil, and Dante without special training. If you can imagine that, you can begin to feel what it is like to be Chinese.

Because of this continuity with ancient times, the Chinese tend to think of the rest of the world's cultures as terribly young. So the rest of the world appears amazingly immature and dangerously unstable. In contrast, Chinese culture, despite its many problems, seems stable and enduring. This perception is deeply connected to the central quest of Chinese philosophy—to honor the unity that transcends difference. This quest for unity affects every part of Chinese life, including its religion—if indeed one can actually distinguish Chinese religion from its philosophy.

As for what Westerners call Chinese religion, the Chinese people have traditionally followed the influence of three major thinkers: Confucius, Lao Tzu, and the Buddha. These men differed one from the other in many ways. They also differed from the popular spiritual practices of the Chinese masses. Nonetheless, they each heavily influenced Chinese culture. Rather than divide China into rival religions, their influences worked to create paradox and subtlety within the Chinese, both as individuals and as a culture.

As a brief explanation of how this works, we can say that Confucius was concerned about how community functions. He wanted each member of the community to know his or her place and be able to carry out his or her given responsibility. Thus, each member of a family would know his or her respective place, each family would know how to carry out its role within the empire, and the people would know how they are connected to their ancestors. This social harmony would create stability and continuity, allowing wisdom to flourish. Confucianism is thus the default theory of government for China. Whether in agreement or opposition, China's government is always reacting to Confucius.

Lao Tzu, the Taoist, taught that one should discover the great Harmony of the cosmos and live in unity with it. Taoists actually thought that not much would come from the Confucian efforts to transform the world. They thought it was better to just let things be, an approach they called "Wu Wei." The Beatles popularized this idea in their song "Let It Be." Taoism is thus the default philosophy for the Chinese individual who searches for meaning within and connection to the natural world.

The Buddha was not Chinese, of course, but once his teachings reached China, Buddhism became an important and enduring part of Chinese culture. Chinese Buddhism concerned itself with nonattachment, principally through meditation, and gradually became the school of thought Chinese call "Ch'an" and Japanese call "Zen." (Whether these are religions or philosophies, I'll leave it to you to judge.) Buddhism became something like China's default psychology.

At the grassroots level, these three streams of thought wove together with the popular spiritual notions of the Chinese people. The mixture created a culture in which it is difficult to know where shamanism ends and philosophy begins, difficult to know the difference between social theory and spirituality. Atheism and animism are not rigidly separate categories in China. In practice, ancient Chinese people often practiced divination, exorcism, spirit writing, and so forth—bringing order to a universe they believed to be populated by ghosts, spirits, and their ancestors—whatever religion or even atheistic philosophy they otherwise claimed to follow.

We don't have time to go into all of that today, of course. My time is limited. So I'll now focus on what I believe Taoism in particular, and Chinese philosophies in general, have to offer Western culture.

A Living Continuity

First, the Chinese way offers people a living continuity with their past and with their present culture. Western culture desperately needs these things right now. American culture is especially vulnerable to the notion that anything old is obsolete. We tend to encourage individuals to isolate themselves from any broader context. We begin new buildings by tearing down old ones. We move far away from home for

the great harmony

economic reasons, unplugging ourselves from all that has come before and from any responsibility for what comes after us.

As for our connection with the past, what young American child now wants to memorize the Gettysburg address, much less learn about the Magna Carta? Of what value are such "ancient" things when compared with the wonders of new technological gadgets? This, I propose, represents great cultural poverty and a profound spiritual emptiness.

In the end, our culture will not be able to survive our plunge into trivia. Trees die when we sever them from their roots. So do individuals and cultures.

A Philosophy of Aesthetics

Second, Chinese wisdom offers a philosophy of aesthetics, called "feng shui," through which we can bring human life and culture into harmony with nature. For example, a builder using the principles of feng shui can consider how the shadows of his proposed building will affect the surrounding buildings at different parts of the day. He can ask whether a nearby mountain or river can influence the placement of the building. Feng shui can influence where the windows of the new building should be. The builder can also decorate the interior in ways that encourage the flow of helpful energy. Feng shui is in short an aesthetic that promotes emotional and physical well-being.

The noted American architect Christopher Alexander drew his inspiration from Taoism. His influential book *The Timeless Way of Building* makes the claim that every culture has its own deeply ingrained "pattern language." When we honor it, our buildings and communities naturally resonate with our culture's deepest values.

Alexander says that because we have been ignoring our pattern language for nearly a half century, architecture has become increasingly disconnected from the people's deepest sense of values.

The movement Alexander birthed—New Urban Development—encourages urban planners to return to traditional Western patterns for designing their streets and buildings. I like Alexander's work. I believe that a person of any faith can profit from Taoist influences just as Alexander has, without any compromise to their own beliefs. After all, Taoism merely seeks to lead people back into the deepest values of their own culture and those of the universe itself. Therefore, one does not have to convert from anything or to anything to profit from Taoist thought.

A Medicine of Prevention

Third, I would suggest that Chinese medicine offers something valuable to Western culture. Briefly, Chinese medicine aims at prevention rather than cure. It seeks to strengthen health rather than to solve medical emergencies.

The practice of Chinese medicine is based on centuries of observation. So one does not have to subscribe to the medical explanations of ancient Chinese doctors to benefit from the cures they developed. It is enough that these cures seem to work and, as the Hippocratic Oath proscribes, they "do no harm."

Still, the theory and practice of traditional Chinese medicine is fascinating and derives logically from Taoist principles.

The ancient Chinese saw the human body as a miniature world. Inside that world were oceans, rivers, canals, deserts, swamps, and so forth. Thus, the human body experiences summers and winters, famines, and earthquakes. The ancient doctors also discovered that our bodies have channels, called "meridians," through which our life force (or "ch'i") flows. Too much (or too little) ch'i causes heat, cold, or damp. Such conditions invite disease. The ancient Chinese developed acupuncture to help direct the ch'i and to encourage healing, gently and naturally.

Nowadays, a Chinese medical practitioner may prescribe a certain diet because specific foods affect the organs of the body in different ways. Herbs too assist the body's natural healing process by regulating its energy, moisture, heat, and so forth.

Explaining how Chinese medicine works is difficult when we use the language of Western science. So far, we have not been able to discover a physical entity that corresponds to a meridian, for example. Nonetheless, acupuncture does work, and it functions according to the descriptions of meridian maps from ancient China. It must work; a number of hospitals across our country are now using acupuncture for pain treatment and other ailments! Even Vanderbilt, a prestigious hospital in Nashville, Tennessee, is building a clinic for the practice of Asian medicine.

You are certain to hear more about Chinese medicine in the days ahead. In our age of runaway medical costs, even the American middle class is frightened about getting sick. So we desperately need a system of affordable health care that focuses on prevention. Chinese medicine offers this.

A Means for Personal Guidance

Finally, the Chinese worldview offers a means for personal guidance. The traditional English word for this is "divination." However, that word is too loaded with negative connotations for followers of Western religions. So I'll try to give a more earthy and practical English explanation for this very Eastern practice.

The Chinese routinely consult works such as the I Ching when making important life decisions. This practice is deeply woven into their traditional culture. Far from being mere superstition or some consultation with diabolical powers, the practice is based upon what Karl Jung called "synchronicity," or the tendency for things related to one another to emerge at the time we need them.

For example, have you ever answered the phone, only to hear the voice of someone you were just thinking about? Have you ever left your house in the morning perplexed, thinking about some decision you must make? Then, as you drive to work you notice a billboard and realize that its message offers new insight into your problem? You could say that a billboard helped you make a decision. You probably wouldn't call it witchcraft!

Here is another example: Have you ever encountered a new idea and then suddenly met some new friends who helped you understand that idea? This phenomena—the tendency for things to converge to give you guidance and helpful information—is what Jung meant by "synchronicity." It happens to everyone who pays attention to life, in every culture and in every religion.

The I Ching is a collection of short commentaries created to help us take advantage of synchronicity. These commentaries are attached to a pattern of marks called "hexagrams," which consist of 64 lines arranged in all their possible configurations. A person seeking guidance from the I Ching begins his or her search with a random selection of patterns; this is often done now by tossing three coins of equal value. The various combinations—three heads, two heads and one tails, two tails and one heads, and so forth—direct the seeker to the appropriate hexagrams. Tossing the coins several times generates phrases and sentences from the commentaries that suggest likely consequences of specific actions.

The Chinese believe that the I Ching works as it does because of invisible lines of power and influence running through the cosmos, the human body, and the social world. These lines continually converge and detach to create the patterns that influence our moods, our abilities, and our opportunities. The I Ching is a device—there are others—that Chinese people believe make such patterns visible and usable.

In my opinion, instruments like the I Ching are based on phenomena that are very real. Although people must discern what to do with this knowledge once they have it, they are still ahead of the game if the process of "Te" (the power of the cosmos) becomes visible.

I hope this broad outline helps introduce you to ancient Chinese thought. China is a rising world power. For us to understand the roots of Chinese culture makes a lot of sense. Even though modern China has been considerably influenced by Western values, at its heart it is still China. In modernized and secularized forms, the basic ideas I have presented to you continue to mold the thoughts and choices of the Chinese people.

The group applauded politely as James took a drink of water from the glass on the stand. He then signaled that he was prepared to receive questions from his audience. He didn't have to wait long.

"James," a man in his mid to late thirties began, "I really enjoyed your presentation."

Thanks.

"Please introduce yourself as you make your comments," Glen interjected.

"My name is Fred Rodriguez," the man said. "I serve as an elder at the Bible Way Community Church in Glendale, Arizona, not far from here. I don't mean to be offensive, James; however, I feel that you have deliberately given us a secular and Western picture of a religion that in reality is filled with mystical beliefs and practices that would curl the hair of most Westerners, Christian or not."

How so?

"Well, I went to China recently with a missions group from my church. Before I went, I checked out some library books about traditional Chinese religion. In one of those books, I read an account from a European anthropologist who had witnessed a public exorcism in a small Chinese village.

the great harmony

He claims that the village elders placed two chairs in front of the town hall for the deities they expected to descend for the meeting. At some point, the antropologist says, those chairs began to shake and bounce—he likened it to a Ouija game. One of the chairs even dipped its leg into ink and began to write on a large piece of paper; it was a decree from the Great Jade Emperor, commanding the demons to leave the town.

"The anthropologist offered no explanation for what he had witnessed, but he claims that the chairs moved from that building out into the town. As this happened, the people went into an ecstatic state.

"So when you talk about the I Ching and make it sound like reading the *Wall Street Journal,* I am recalling that story. From a Christian standpoint, practices like using the I Ching or inviting deities to descend for a village meeting involve communication with a world that we view as dark and dangerous. I think it slightly dishonest to talk about Taoism and Chinese religion as though they are more like philosophical systems than spiritual practices and supernatural phenomena forbidden by our Scripture."

I don't take offense at your comment. Chinese culture has always allowed for phenomena such as you have described. For the educated person, however, the deities and apparently supernatural phenomena to which you refer are metaphors and symbols for abstract ideas and natural energies. In fact, I first learned this from my Methodist pastor, Dr. Samuelson, when I was just a teenager. He had been influenced by the writings of Karl Jung at Emory University and taught a class on Jung in our church.

Now, I am not a psychologist, but if I am correct, Jung believed that every human being shares a "collective unconscious" with everyone who has ever lived on the planet. Primal ideas and images, called "archetypes," emerge from this collective unconscious and so are common to people everywhere. The archetypes appear to us in dreams and visions. People through the ages (and all over the world) have depicted them in their art. Images of Madonna and child, grandfather, the temptress, the tempter, and so forth are examples of such archetypes. What you were describing in that town meeting in rural China was simply the way unlettered and uneducated people express spiritual and psychological reality. Educated people, whether in China or elsewhere, would probably express these archetypal images and emotions differently.

As for being "slightly dishonest," Taoists are not the only ones learning to present their ideas in modern and nonthreatening ways. Recently, I attended a Christian church in Los Angeles with my cousin. I was surprised to see that there was no cross, no Communion table, no religious symbolism of any kind. The music sounded like secular tunes from the late eighties. In his sermon, the preacher actually ridiculed old Christian hymns and catechism.

As I recall, the Christian Bible contains numerous accounts of exorcism and other kinds of supernatural stuff, but I saw none of that in this self-confessed conservative Christian church. In fact, I am of the opinion that these sorts of ancient things would be slightly embarrassing to the people whose church I attended. I don't think that makes them dishonest though; it just makes them modern people.

There were a number of other questions before the session ended, but the one from the Christian guy really caught my attention. Most of the others asked for clarifications about Taoist practices or Chinese medicine. James told a lady who asked about his training that he had attended graduate school in San Francisco at a place called the Institute for Integral Studies, although it had been called the Institute of Asian Studies when he attended. I looked it up later and discovered that it is a fully accredited school for psychology and sociology students. Anyway, James went from there to Taipei, where he studied Chinese language and Chinese medicine for three more years.

When Glen announced that we needed to move on and should take a brief break, I noticed that the tension that had at first filled the room was turning into genuine interest and curiosity.

JOURNAL NOTES

So, what did I learn about Taoism? How do I view it though Christian and biblical eyes?

First, some positive things.

Taoism's talk about "the way" is a powerful testimony to the idea that God's law is embedded in creation itself. Romans 1 says as much. So does Psalm 8. God is the Lord of all, and His creation reflects His values and character. In fact, C.S. Lewis used the word "Tao" in *Mere Christianity* to describe the natural sense of right and wrong that is built within creation.

(The theory of natural law, important to Western Christian jurisprudence, rests on that idea.)

Practically speaking, the universe does seem to have a "grain." My father taught me years ago that when working with wood, working with the grain is easier than working against it. When we honor the grain, things tend to go well. When we don't, the going can get rough. Perhaps my father's insight is the basic idea of Taoism—find the grain!

In all sorts of activities, from sports to sex, we experience joy when we "go with the flow." The Taoists have turned this truth into a profound and nuanced philosophy. Therefore we can learn much from Taoism, whether in medicine, decorating, or governance. More specifically, the Tao Te Ching offers much and offends rarely. A Christian can certainly reflect on its teachings without comprising his or her faith. Actually, the Tao Te Ching is not much different from our books of Proverbs and Ecclesiastes. In fact, the book of Ecclesiastes calls our faith into question far more than the Tao Te Ching does!

On the other hand, the Bible, beginning in Genesis, teaches us that natural is not enough. Because we are fallen creatures, our nature is flawed. Therefore, fallen nature often leads us to wrong conclusions. St. Paul affirms that nature is a witness to God's glory and character, but he reminds us that our ancestors—who were more in touch with nature than we are—did not retain their understanding of God. They became "vain in their imaginations."[1] For this reason, God abandoned them to the desires of their fallen nature, and as a result, they became idolatrous, immoral, and violent. In other words, Paul was saying that history reveals that the human ability to read nature is terribly flawed.

For all these reasons, Jews and Christians are forbidden to practice divination. We must not attempt to use nature to control the Spirit—that is to say, to practice magic. God may choose to give us supernatural insights as it pleases Him; we must not seek occult knowledge. Neither should we make supernatural phenomenon the focus of our spiritual attention. We are too broken to navigate at that level of spiritual life. Although we live our lives within nature, we must do so according to the knowledge that comes to us from outside and from above nature—the words of Holy Scripture.

Judaism and Christianity therefore differ from Taoism in that they are not natural religions. They are revealed religions.

Our Scriptures claim to be words of the Creator, who spoke through ancient witnesses. These words show us the way to salvation and wholeness.

Certainly, we can gain much from observing nature. We can and should admit that modern Christians have become too detached from nature, even from human nature. Nonetheless, Taoism offers a way that is impossible for fallen human beings to follow. It offers a view of nature based on a denial of the fall. It presupposes that nature is whole, that we are capable of understanding nature's lessons, and that we can live in a way that is consistent with what we learn from nature. Christians have historically disagreed with all three of these claims.

The universe is "red in tooth and claw," as Tennyson put it. The world is out of sorts, not quite itself, bent. We share this condition with the rest of the universe; we too are fallen. Our intellect is fallen: We come to wrong conclusions about God. Our emotions are fallen: We can be deeply attached to things that are wrong or even evil. Our drives are fallen: We often crave things that are wicked. Furthermore, even when we know what things we ought to do, we often lack the ability to do those things. We get addicted, hijacked, and twisted. St. Paul repeatedly reminds us of this.

So we need more than nature; we need law to reveal our true condition and prescribe a remedy.

However, even law does not do the trick. Our ability to carry out law is also broken. That's why we also need grace.

Grace is God's power and favor. Grace makes us acceptable to God before we even begin our spiritual journey. Grace also gives us the power for transformation so we can live according to God's plan for our lives.

Taoism does not seem to understand our need for grace. How can it? It fails to experience human beings as broken creatures. In short, Taoism describes the world as it was before the fall and as it will be when the curse is finally lifted.

If we have no need of grace, we have no need for the Christ who died to give us grace. Therefore, Taoism has no place for Jesus as Son of God and Savior of the world.

I picked up a copy of the Gospel of John the other day that had been translated from Chinese. I decided to buy it because of the commentary that was printed side by side with the Gospel readings. I was shocked to read the first verses of the first chapter: "In the Beginning was the Tao. The Tao was with God and the Tao was God…and the Tao became flesh and dwelt among us."

The attached commentary said something like this: "Tao is the Chinese equivalent of the Greek word 'logos.' The logos is the way, the pattern, and the foundation of all that is. Clearly in his introduction of Jesus to the Greeks, St. John intended to bridge the gap between Hebrew and Greek thought. He wanted to tell us that Jesus, not nature, was the expressed image of the invisible God. Jesus is the way that leads from a fallen world back to God the Father."

The Tao as a Chinese equivalent of logos…interesting! That made me think further about what this implied.

Lao Tzu claimed that the Tao cannot be named, and therein lies our central difference with Taoism. A Christian believes that the Tao *can* be named; it is the name above every name, the name at which every knee shall bow and every tongue confess. The Tao, the truth, and the life is a person: Jesus Christ, begotten before all worlds, light of light, God of God, truly God and truly man.

the rivers all flow into one ocean:
the allure of hinduism

They call Him Indra, Mitra, Agni.
They call Him Garutman.
They call Him Yama and Matarishvan.
There is One God; He is known by many names.

The dark-skinned man stood quietly at the front of the room. He wore khaki pants, a dark blue blazer, and an oxford button-down cloth shirt. He seemed slightly ill-at-ease, as though he was not sure he had done the right thing by dressing that casually. He had, after all, decided not to wear his customary tie today. Still, he seemed likeable enough. For some reason, he made me think of Mr. Rogers.

When he began to speak, his English was only slightly influenced by that lyric sound that Americans have come to expect from English-speaking people raised in India. His vocabulary revealed him to be a man of great intelligence and dignity. Something in him seemed larger than his rather small stature.

Good afternoon. My real name is Kavi Menon Upadhyaya, but my classmates back in England always called me Carl Updike.

There is no real story about how I got my English name. A young Irish gentleman at my boarding school in Thiruvananthapuram first gave it to me the week I enrolled there. Then, the name followed me on to the University of London. So rest assured, I will answer to "Carl" if you cannot pronounce (or cannot remember) my Indian name.

I was invited to talk to you today about the world's oldest continuing religion. Although I must warn you from the outset that I am no expert on the subject, I am not sure anyone is an expert. At any rate, Hinduism is not about words; it's about a way of seeing the world. It is a way of living one's life. With that in mind, I will do my best to tell you something about the beliefs and practices of what the Western world calls "Hinduism."

I am a little surprised to be here. I am not a priest or a religious teacher. I happen to be a pediatrician, presently living in Biloxi, Mississippi, where I have practiced medicine for three years. I was born in India. My parents sent me to a boarding school on the outskirts of London to prepare me for university. Afterward, I went to the University of London and from there to complete my medical studies at Cambridge.

For most of my young adulthood, I enthusiastically embraced a secular and Western point of view. I only gradually and reluctantly became interested in the philosophical and spiritual traditions of my homeland. As the years went by, I began to understand that life would simply not hold up under the "unbearable lightness of being" that is the shadow side of Western secular culture.

Two important experiences awakened my interest in Vedanta, or the study of India's ancient scripture. The first was when I read Milan Kundera's famous novel, to which I have just referred—*The Unbearable Lightness of Being*. I read it twice. Then I saw the movie based on the book. As I thought about why the book and the movie had affected me so deeply, I became aware that Kundera had exposed the utter poverty of Western culture, detached as it has become from both its classical and religious foundations. The Western world, or so it seemed to me, was whirling furiously around a black hole of soullessness. Furthermore, that seemed to be the condition of my own being.

The second experience occurred while I was taking a physics course at the University of London. It was called "Beyond Newton: Exploring the philosophical implications of modern physics." I was in pre-med studies at the time. However, I felt that I should broaden my understanding of other fields for my own personal enrichment. The course had been created for people like me who wanted to understand, at least superficially, what the theories of relativity and quantum mechanics actually address and imply.

The twentieth-century discoveries in physics were arguably the greatest philosophical revelations of all time. They revealed that the nature of reality is more like the description one encounters in our

ancient Vedas than the one we learned from the European Enlightenment. (My professor actually said this!) The reality described by
relativity at the level of the stars and galaxies, and the reality described
by quantum mechanics at the level of subatomic matter—these turned
the materialistic view of modern Western culture on its head. We
learned that the universe behaves very differently from the way Western thinkers since Aristotle have believed.

This revolution in the field of physics has caused convulsions through
every level of the Western world. Western culture has reacted with
a deep sense of cynicism. (In fact, this is what postmodernism is: an
outrage against the betrayal of Western philosophy against itself.) This
cynicism, however, cannot last.

Postmodernism is a kind of cultural despair, a sense of Western
defeat for having not been correct about profound things. Anyway, as
I learned more about the discoveries of the Western physicists, I was
startled to realize that Indian thinkers had come to these same conclusions ages ago. In fact, Indians have been laughing about the naïveté of
common sense for centuries.

So I decided that I needed to know more about the ancient Indian
thinkers who had come to the conclusions about reality Western scientists are only now discovering.

I began my studies of Vedanta like any Westerner might—by reading books about the Vedas written specifically for Western people. Two
helpful ones were *The Wisdom of the Vedas* by J.C. Chatterji and *Vedanta:
the Voice of Freedom* by Swami Vivekananda. Both of these books were
written early in the twentieth century to explain the view of reality
proposed by the Vedas. As I read them, I was seized by something like
awe; I felt that they explained a universe that sounded very much like
what I had learned in my physics class.

In time, I became more serious about meditation and other facets
of spiritual life. (However, I am glad that Hinduism teaches that we are
here for many lifetimes. I think I will need all my lifetimes just to read
the writings we honor as scripture!)

There was polite laughter through the room.

It is difficult to tell you exactly what Hindus believe. If another Hindu
were addressing you today, he or she might say very different things

the **rivers** all flow into **one** ocean

from what I will. Our religion, you see, embraces many different approaches to God, reality, and life.

Hinduism, you might say, is like a great tent; it shelters a wide spectrum of human thought and behavior. What unites our diversity under the simple label "Hinduism" is the common view of reality that our various schools of spirituality embrace.

I have decided for our purposes today to focus on this Hindu view of reality. To do so, I will draw upon the devotional text one is likely to encounter among Hindus of the various schools: the Bhagavad Gita. This will suffice to give you at least a superficial look at our religion in this hour that I have to speak.

Perhaps it will help to tell you that Hinduism revolves around these central ideas:

1. The universe is conscious. All parts of the universe share in this consciousness.

2. Although the various parts of the universe are not really separate from one another and from the whole, these apparent parts of the universe are often ignorant of their underlying oneness.

3. Entities move through various forms as they lose or gain awareness of their authentic nature. Thus, an animal may become a human being or a human being may become a more enlightened person, passing through several lifetimes as the process continues. This process is called reincarnation. (Unfortunately, the process can go in the other direction too; an entity can lose awareness, descending lower and lower into the direction of ignorance.)

4. Entities accumulate or lose merit, or karma, depending upon the choices they make within their given circumstance.

5. The truth about reality is found by raising one's conscious awareness. Becoming aware, or enlightened, helps us gain release from our spiritual exile. Meditation is the core spiritual practice that helps us to do this.

6. There are several paths toward spiritual growth. These include the paths of intellect, devotion, aestheticism, service, and conscious training.

Perhaps it would be helpful to point out that Indian culture does not make the sharp distinction between faith, science, philosophy, and art that Westerners tend to do. Our philosophy has religious implications, our religion offers a context for scientific understanding, our art does not distinguish between myth and dogma. In other words, we search for a seamless connection between the various parts of human existence.

Because of our "big umbrella" approach to study and reflection, the Hindu scriptures often express doubt as well as faith—even about God. One particularly beautiful and moving passage in the Rig Veda goes on for pages about the glory and beauty of the universe as it was being birthed. (It actually reminds me of the opening lines from the book of Genesis.) However, the Hindu passage ends with a line that nearly always shocks Westerners. Let me read it to you.

In the beginning there was neither existence nor nonexistence:
Neither the world nor the sky beyond was...
That One breathed, without breath, by its own impulse;
Other than that was nothing at all...

In the beginning was love,
Which was the primal germ of the mind.
The seers, searching in their hearts with wisdom,
discovered the connection between existence and nonexistence.

These states were divided by a crosswise line.

What was below and what was above?
There were bearers of seed and mighty forces,
Impulse from below and forward movement from above.

Who really knows? Who here can say?
When was this born and from where did it come—this creation?
The gods came later than this world's creation—
Therefore who knows from where creation came?

That out of which creation came,
whether it held it together or did not,
He who sees it in the highest heaven,
Only He knows—or perhaps even He does not know!

I have heard Westerners groan in despair about that final verse! However, to a Hindu the passage merely states the obvious: We have no idea about the events of creation. That doesn't stop us from wondering about them or from writing beautiful verse about them.

Becoming aware of our ignorance should stop us from creating dogma that we cannot substantiate, however.

The Vedas teach us that we can learn about only one thing—ourselves. We cannot go into the heavens—we can only go inward. We can explore the meaning of who we are and what we are. That is the best we can do. Knowing this is true spirituality.

Hinduism is a collection of ideas, scriptures, and practices that may seem contradictory not only to those of other religions but even to other Hindus. We may say then that Hinduism is an attitude about the world more than it is a dogma. It tends to embrace rather than to exclude differences. It does this because Hinduism is an inquiry into the nature of reality and especially into the reality of human consciousness. Therefore, Hindu inclusion does not stop even at the borders of Hinduism—if such borders even exist. It includes all.

In my father's little village is a temple that I have visited several times. Inside the temple is a statue of Christ. Except for the fact that Christ is painted blue (out of respect for His divine origin), the statue is recognizable as the man Christians believe to be God. The statue is there because Hindus have no trouble with the assertion that Christ is God. Therefore, they have no problem praying to Christ. Why should they? Christ is a particularly clear manifestation of the divine for multiplied millions of human beings.

Then again, so are you! And my friend, this is the contribution Hinduism offers to the world: The Buddha, Jesus, Krishna, Rama, Moses, Muhammad, and countless others came to teach us the way to God, or to universal consciousness, if you prefer. All these enlightened souls are worthy of great respect and veneration. However, they became great only because they grasped the truth that the universe and all it contains is one.

Existence is conscious!

Stop a moment and reflect on that: Existence is conscious.

All that exists is a part of that one consciousness, including you and me. Therefore, the quest to know God—or ultimate being, or reality—begins by learning how to recognize and expand the parameters of one's consciousness.

That's the main thing, you see. We have thousands of gods and goddesses in India. On the other hand, we have only one God. Then again, we have no god! We focus upon the aspects of universal mind that help us gain understanding of reality. Shiva offers one aspect of that reality; Krishna another. Respectfully, I say that a rock or a tree will serve as well as any religious painting or statue as a means of focusing our awareness upon ultimate being. Indeed, my own breath is quite sufficient. Therefore, a temple is never more than a breath away. In one moment I can shift my focus away from "maya"—the illusion of permanence—and toward an awareness of the great interconnected nature of being that unites us all to the all.

That is why I meditate. Meditation is a coming home to who we really are. As I focus upon breathing, I begin to sense the rhythm of being that undergirds all things. I remember that I am a part of existence. I remember that I am existence!

That realization can come as quite a shock! Swami Vivekananda used to tell the story about how this realization came to him. Like me, he had a Western education that caused him to be rather contemptuous of Hindu practices and beliefs. In fact, he used to enjoy ridiculing the swamis and sages of India. Then one day, a friend took him to visit a temple in Howrah. When he met the priest, he mockingly challenged the holy man and demanded to be introduced to God! At this, the priest lifted his foot almost to his head, held it there for a moment and then touched the young Westerner's head with his big toe. The young cynic was immediately flooded with bliss and a consciousness of ultimate being. Needless to say, the young man became more respectful of spiritual reality. In fact, he became a very great teacher![1]

In a way, what happened to Vivekananda is a picture of what I believe is happening to Western culture. Right now, the Western world is swinging from skepticism to extreme gullibility. (Perhaps this is an inevitable stage in a culture's spiritual development, but it is certainly an interesting thing to watch from an Eastern perspective.) Sooner or later, Western culture must come to peace with the truth about reality.

Just a few decades ago, Westerners were certain that matter *was* reality. Love, value, courage, sacrifice—all such abstract things were thought to be based on material substances. Love was simply the reproductive urge. Courage was our instinctual urge to preserve the future of our species even at the cost of our individual life. Spirituality was the need to have parents in heaven to take care of our anxious hearts. Biology would soon explain the origins and functions of all our human urges, regardless of how noble or grand. Metaphysical explanations were doomed. Matter was everything.

This extreme commitment to reality as matter was taken for granted by nearly all educated people. So the current revival of spiritual life in the West is as confused and chaotic as it was unexpected. Now, the sublime exists alongside of the ridiculous; saintly spiritual leaders minister alongside of manipulative marketers. The West has become a veritable marketplace of religions and philosophies.

Believe me, I am not mocking Western culture's new spiritual confusion. In India, we have a lot of experience with this sort of religious paradox. However, Hinduism allows us to withhold ultimate judgment, even on the absurd. This allows us to respect what we do not yet understand. Hindus have come to know that sometimes, apparently absurd beliefs or practices contain startling insights. Einstein, you will remember, discovered his principles of relativity while daydreaming about a man riding through space on a beam of light! Friedrich Kekulé discovered the chemical structure of the benzene molecule after he had a dream about a snake biting its own tail. Coleridge wrote Kubla Khan after smoking opium. So you see, even in the skeptical West, discoveries in science and art have not always been the products of cold, calculating reason. As Pascal said in his *Pensees*, "The heart has its reasons that reason does not grasp."

What I am trying to say is that humility is always to be preferred over arrogance. If not, you might get zapped like our famous swami!

At its core, the devotional path of Hinduism is really a deliberate cultivation of humility. We worship our gods and goddesses with the knowledge that they may not be what we imagine them to be—indeed, they may not exist at all in any empirically verifiable way! This allows us to treat other religions as variations of our own. I can easily worship in a Christian church, and I have on many occasions! (I adore the book of Ecclesiastes, by the way. I read it once a year at least.) This, I believe, is a humble way of learning and living.

Devotion is also a cultivation of gratitude. It is a surrender of our certainty, a willingness to live joyfully within the unavoidable ambiguity of a vast and largely unexplainable universe.

I urge you to read the greatest classic of Hindu devotion—the Bhagavad Gita. In Steven Mitchell's English translation, Krishna assures us that "none who truly love me will ever be lost." He doesn't say that all who *understand* him will never be lost, but that all who *love* him will never be lost. Therefore, a Hindu ought to love and respect all aspects of the divine. However, a Hindu must hold lightly to his or her ideological formulations because they are almost certainly false, or at least incomplete.

In the Bhagavad Gita, Krishna descends to comfort and instruct a warrior named Arjuna. The man is about to go into battle, and naturally he is terrified. But Arjuna is frightened not because he may die but because he may kill. Krishna comforts him by saying that all outward things change. Therefore, to find peace, Arjuna must move beyond his attachment to appearances and discover the things in himself that are unchangeable. As the Gita puts it,

> These bodies come to an end;
> But that vast embodied Self
> Is ageless, fathomless, and eternal.[2]

So I leave you with this. Our ancient thinkers pictured reality in a way that is very similar to the description in the wonderful movie *The Thirteenth Floor*. In that movie, the creators of a computer game can enter and exit their game at will. While they are in the game, they experience the universe they have created as concrete reality. Only when they exit the game do they remember that their momentary perception of reality has been provincial and temporary. As the movie progresses, they discover something else: The world in which they live their "real" lives is itself a simulation. Other beings are also descending at will into *their* world to alter *their* reality.

The Thirteenth Floor leaves us wondering how far down and how far up these layers of reality go or whether any ultimate ground of being exists.

Hinduism says that the question of whether there is an ultimate reality—a ground of being—is unanswerable. We can only know that the appearances of our known world are deceiving; the universe is not as real as we experience it. Gods from other places may indeed descend and ascend as they please. However, the gods too are parts of the same unknowable ultimate existence. To know this fully is to step out from the endless pain of separation from the one. It is to enter into the bliss of ultimate union. This is the essence of Hinduism.

JOURNAL NOTES

Wow! I have to admit, these other religions would be easier to deal with if I didn't like the people who follow them! Perhaps that is why religious people through history have felt the need to whip up their emotions against people of other religions.

Some of the world's bloodiest conflicts sprang from religious rivalry. Didn't the Christians of St. Chrysostom's time burn a synagogue full of Jews? As a Christian I shudder at such a thing. It happened, though. Christians probably somehow ceased to view Jews as people made in God's image and likeness. Do we still do this?

I think I have had a childhood image of Hindus as poor superstitious people starving to death while cows walk around their town. Well, that won't work! Dr. Upadhyaya is anything but ignorant. Furthermore, I found myself agreeing with him about the "unbearable lightness of being" that our culture has embraced. I have experienced the vacuum he is talking about. We seem to have steadily eliminated the sense of the holy from everything in our culture—even from our religion. Sometimes, our culture feels as though it has no core.

I also found myself agreeing with Dr. Upadhyaya's idea that discoveries in physics have spiritual implications. More and more Western believers are going to have enormous problems with the view of reality that these discoveries suggest. However, I think that we have these problems not because our faith is shaking but because our culture is shaking. The extent that we have identified our faith with our culture is the extent to which our faith will seem to be shaking. Nonetheless, many Western Christians are going to become increasingly uncomfortable because educated people can no longer view reality in the way Westerners have traditionally viewed it.

On the other hand, Christians from the second century would not feel comfortable with the way we modern American Christians have dismissed supernatural things—such as angelic visitations, for example. That tells us that our faith has already survived great cultural shifts.

Didn't St. Paul tell us not to forget to receive strangers because some of us had "entertained angels unawares?"[3] How many *modern* conservative American Christians take that passage literally? (Here's another question: Why do educated Christians in other cultures still take these passages literally?)

The truth is, Western conservatives are as infected by the extreme material view of the universe as are liberal Christians. This means that early Christians—and many Christians in other cultures today—would experience the world more like Hindus do than the way Western Christians experience it.

This is what makes many Christians uncomfortable with the presence of other religions in our country. We have lost much of our own spiritual knowledge. We desperately need to recover knowledge of our own Scripture and theology to operate in this new (but actually ancient) environment.

On the other hand, even though the Hindus have not accepted the West's material way of looking at the world, they have embraced a spirituality that no Christian—Western or not—can embrace. Our Scriptures do not allow us to think of matter as unreal or even as a lesser reality. We cannot believe that the universe is conscious or that we are all parts of ultimate being. Therefore, we are at odds with Hinduism at profound levels.

We believe that God created things in a way that grants to those things a dependent but a very real existence.

God has given human beings the ability to become *persons*—beings with a self-directed potential to choose a relationship with Him and with one another. Although our capacity for relationship was damaged by the fall, God offers restoration and relationship through Christ. Because of this, relationship with God calls us to an even fuller sort of personhood. We ultimately will become eternal companions of the Almighty. One cannot be a companion if he or she is not a separate person.

Therefore, we do not seek to merge with God; we seek to become friends of God. In return, God offers to grant us wholeness and eternal personhood.

Jesus Christ is, for us, the pattern for what we will become. As St. John put it, "We shall be like Him, for we shall see Him as He is."[4] Unlike Krishna, Christ was not only apparently a man. Jesus was God who actually became a man. That's why painting a statue of Christ blue violates the incarnation, even if Hindus do it to show respect for Christ's divinity. Jesus was God, who "emptied Himself" and "made Himself of no reputation."[5] He was not God in a coat of flesh; he was God who became man in every respect.

As a man, Jesus Christ becomes a model of what every man and woman can become. God descended to earth so that we could ascend to heaven. Christ is now at the right hand of God, and God has "seated us with Him in the heavenly places in Christ."[6] We have an intimacy with God that does not require us to disappear. We are real persons and are becoming ever more real as we grow in Christ.

We also differ from Hindus in the way we view supernatural phenom-enon. Like many other spiritual paths, Hinduism believes that one can learn to control spiritual forces. Christians believe in the gifts of the Holy Spirit, which on occasion can be spectacular and otherworldly. However, God gives these gifts "according to His own will" and not according to human will.[7] Paul and Silas did not create an earthquake by concentrating their mental energies. God sent an earthquake to get His friends out of jail. God chose not to send an earthquake to free John the Baptist. We don't know why. We only know that the power of God is under His sovereignty. God asks us to trust Him as He does what pleases Him. Therefore, we can humbly make requests, but we cannot control supernatural forces.

Hindus worship some archetypal images that Christians regard as demonic. That seems harsh, but it is the unavoidable truth. We do not believe that evil is the shadow side of God. We believe that evil is a part of creation that resists God. Furthermore, evil is headquartered within spiritual entities called demons. Some of the Hindu deities have attributes that the Bible describes as belonging to these demonic forces.

For all these reasons, a Christian cannot worship the Hindu pantheon or otherwise participate in a Hindu worship service. We may respectfully observe the rites of Hindu friends, such as weddings and so forth, but we cannot say the prayers or participate in the spiritual life of a Hindu temple. We realize that our exclusivity may seem brutal and uncharitable to our Hindu friends. This should move us to be more diligent about showing through our lives that we do not intend any disrespect. We should create venues for meeting with Hindus so we can discuss our differences and otherwise work to make genuine relationships with them. After all, our God is a God of reconciliation. That means that we must be a people of reconciliation. We cannot, however, ignore the theological boundaries that separate and define our respective religions.

We believe that the Holy Spirit, who wooed us even when we were yet "dead in trespasses and sins," is at work in those who follow the ways of ancient India.[8] He woos Hindus just as He has wooed us because God longs that Hindus too come to the knowledge of the one who "became flesh and dwelt among us…the only begotten of the Father, full of grace and truth."[9]

the end of suffering:
following the buddha
in the surrender of self

As the shadow follows the body;
as we think, so we become.

The petite woman with dancing eyes looked around at her audience and began to sing:

Row, row, row your boat gently down the stream;
Merrily, merrily, merrily, merrily, life is but a dream!

Then she laughed and began her presentation:

Perhaps I first became a Buddhist when my grandmother taught me that song. Like many important things, the truth about everything was in that little children's song. If we allow them to, the words can shatter the illusions that cause all our pain. Life is indeed but a dream. Things go a lot better for us when we learn to row, row, row our boats gently down the stream of time.

Okay, that's really heavy! Let me tell you a joke.

A policeman is dispatched to a house to investigate a mugging. He knocks on the door and is surprised when a snail answers. Nonetheless, he takes out his notepad and begins to ask his usual questions: "When did the mugging occur? What did the assailant look like? How long did you wait to call the police?"

The snail tries to cooperate but soon begins to sob uncontrollably.

"It was a turtle," the snail manages to say between sobs.

"Very well," the policeman replies kindly. "Try to remember what the turtle looked like."

At this the snail weeps and shakes for a few minutes and finally is able to say, "I don't remember! It all happened so fast!"

When she finished her joke, the speaker began to laugh again. Her laughter was as delightful as it was unexpected and soon became contagious. Everyone in the room got caught up in the utter silliness of the mood.

Don't you see? Our interpretation of life brings us joy or suffering, not the events themselves. We have been laughing because a snail's perception of time is so different from ours. To the snail, however, the turtle's hostile actions appeared to take place in a whirlwind of aggression.

So who is right, us or the snail?

Now this is not just a silly joke. In our everyday lives, we often discover differences in perception. What do we do with them?

Several years ago, I was teaching a semester at McGill University in Montreal. I had a student there who was an Inuit from above the arctic circle. He complained to me several times because the Quebec government had assigned him to the same apartment as an immigrant from Cambodia. In early March, the Inuit man wanted to raise the windows of the apartment to let in the fresh, warm, 40-degree air. The Cambodian, on the other hand, wanted to turn up the heat!

One way of looking at their dilemma is to say that each was causing the suffering of the other. But from a Buddhist perspective, what actually caused the suffering was the different definition of "normal" to which each man was clinging.

Oh, I forgot to tell you who I am! That might help before I get too deep into my topic today.

On the other hand, what can I tell you about who I am? Do I describe to you my perception of myself? Do I tell you how my students view me? I have cousins who last saw me fifteen years ago. Their picture of me will be quite different from what you are likely to perceive. So do I describe myself as my cousins experience me? Which of the pictures of myself do I offer you?

My name is Torri Adams. I have become who I appear to be to you (and even to myself) by telling myself a story. I tend to be highly invested in this story. If your perception of me does not match with the story, or if your definition of reality does not match the one to which I cling, I can get anxious, afraid, or even hostile. Something in me desperately wants my story to be true and universal.

In other words, the sense of who I am is constructed. It comes from my private story about myself. It emerges from a collective story that my family and culture gave to me. It continues to develop as I form interpretations of the events I face in life. It evolves as I retell those events and as I continually reshape my remembrance of them. My story, therefore, is not fixed—it is not solid.

My personal story begins in ambiguity. Race is an important category in our country, so I felt forced to draw a conclusion about who I was, racially speaking, as an adolescent. Making the decision about my race thus became a vital part of creating my sense of self. Today, my choice seems obvious, but I can imagine having arrived at very different conclusions had I decided to label myself differently.

My mother was the daughter of Japanese immigrants to Hawaii. They spoke Japanese in their home, so I grew up with a familiarity with the language. However, my mother rarely spoke Japanese. She spoke, dressed, and thought as an American in every way. She respected my grandparents and sometimes went to the temple with them for special occasions, but she was definitely an American.

My father, on the other hand, was raised in Allentown, Pennsylvania. He was the son of a Presbyterian minister. Dad enlisted in the United States Navy and got stationed in Hawaii. That's where he met my mother. They got married, and I came along three years later. We lived in Hawaii until I was twelve, the year my dad got out of the Navy and got a job that transferred him to Stockton, California.

That move immediately challenged my early stories about myself.

In Hawaii, a lot of kids looked like me, so I didn't need to decide whether I was Japanese or Anglo. I was a natural part of a collective story that encouraged me to think of myself as just another American kid. However, when we moved to Stockton, people pushed me to define myself. I had to come up with a new story about who I was. At first, I did this to satisfy them. But at a deeper level, I did it to satisfy myself. I had never called myself a Japanese-American before. But after some particularly painful experiences at school and at the Presbyterian church we sometimes attended, I began to profess pride in my Asian heritage. I began to call my grandparents much more often. I tried to speak Japanese. When I visited Hawaii, I wanted to go to the temple, where there were other Japanese-Americans.

In reaction to the racial preoccupation of my schoolmates—and of the larger society—I had created a new story for myself.

Was my story true? It seems true to me now. However, it only became true because I created the story and decided to make it my own.

I was trying to run away from the pain of being different. I craved the company of the kids at school and church. I needed a reason for my differences. So it was my reaction to suffering and craving that pushed me toward a different path than I might have otherwise chosen. This is how our stories always evolve at both the individual and the collective levels. We cannot avoid having a story, but we do damage to ourselves when we treat these stories as anything but stories.

What happens to us when we began to see our stories as mere reactions to our suffering and craving? What happens when we learn to view our precious stories about ourselves as mere dreams?

That is what happened to me while I was living for a year with my great aunt in Sapporo, Japan. She was a part of a Buddhist sect that some people call "Pure Land." I was moved by the practices I learned while visiting with her and began to go deeper into the "dharma"—the teaching—of enlightenment. I experienced the joy of abandoning the insistence that my story about myself and the world was in any way objectively true. I began to see the world as a movie, a dream, a drama of my own making.

The man we call the Buddha had a similar experience about five hundred years before the birth of Christ. Because he was born a prince, his father had the necessary wealth and power to shield him from the harsher realities of life. One day, though, the young Siddhartha Gautama (later in life called Shakyamuni, or "sage of the Shaka family") wandered away from the wealthy compound of his father's estate. He saw an old man, a sick person, a dead body, and a beggar. These experiences burst his bubble of innocence. The world, as it turned out, was very different from how he had imagined it to be.

After that, Shakyamuni couldn't put his old world back together. Now we might say that he had experienced a trauma and that his continuing preoccupation with suffering was an example of post-traumatic stress. (That's an example, by the way, of an entirely new plot in our cultural story that we have learned to tell ourselves in order to process difficult things.) However we tell the story of Siddhartha, we know that the trauma he experienced destroyed his capacity to keep deceiving himself. His old story was now shattered.

He had to find out what life was about. That's why he left his new wife and son to go out into the world and to live as a monk.

For some time, he deprived himself of pleasures and afflicted himself with austerities. Then one day, nearly dead from starvation and exposure, he decided that he was no closer to reality than before. He was just poorer. So he sat down under a tree and began to meditate on all he had learned. That's when he became the enlightened one, that is to say, the Buddha.

He had learned that neither indulgence nor deprivation could make one holy. What held people back from truth or joy was not food, sex, and other pleasures, but ignorance of the true nature of reality and of self.

Until he was eighty years old, Shakyamuni taught the dharma to his disciples. This teaching began to spread through the countries of Asia, gradually becoming the various schools of thought and practice that we call Buddhism today.

Because our time is brief, I won't try to define the various schools of Buddhist practice. However, the schools can be broadly categorized by how the faith spread through Asia. Northern Asian countries—Nepal, Tibet, Mongolia, Korea, China, and Japan—tend to follow varieties of Mahayana Buddhism. People in the southern countries usually follow Theravada Buddhism, sometimes called Himayana in older texts. (That label is considered insulting now.)

Each culture where Buddhism has spread has influenced its ideas and practices. That's why Buddhists often use different terms to refer to the same ideas or practices. I tend to use Japanese or Chinese terms; others will use the Tibetan, Pali, or Sanskrit terms, depending on their particular training. As Buddhism has taken deeper root in the West, we are beginning to develop a spiritual vocabulary of our own that is helping us to communicate with our non-Buddhist friends.

Lama Surya Das, born in New York as Jeffrey Miller, has written an excellent and enjoyable book for those of you who want to know more about Buddhism. It is called *Awaken the Buddha Within*, published by Broadway Books. It is written from a Tibetan perspective but also gives an excellent overview of the beliefs and practices of Buddhism in general. I think you would find it full of wisdom for life, whether or not you intend to become a Buddhist.

Okay, let me tell you a cute story.

Some friends of mine have a little girl; she's four years old now. Anyway, the other night they were talking about change and about how we tend to resist it. Suddenly, little Sophia announced, "I'm going to change. I'm going to put on my princess pajamas!"

They laughed and went on talking as Sophia went into her room. In short order, she came out of her room completely naked with her hands resting on her hips. Her mother, wondering what was going on remarked, "Sophia, you are naked!"

"Yes," the girl replied. "To change you must first get naked!"

And that, my friends, is the first principle of Buddhism. Well, almost. It is not so much that we must get naked but that we must recognize that we are already naked. Not only are we naked as individuals, we are naked as cultures. Actually, even the entire universe is naked! The emperor, as we learned as children, has no clothes!

Life, identity, attachments of all sorts—they're all dreams! Everything is naked.

Understanding this awakens us to the reality of what we call the four noble truths:

1. Life is difficult and filled with suffering.

2. The cause of suffering is craving.

3. We bring an end to our suffering by realizing how silly it is for us to crave things in this life. The end of suffering is called "nirvana," which means to "extinguish the fire," or to become wholly satisfied.

4. We can accomplish this state of satisfaction by following a certain path. The path has eight components:

Wisdom

1. Right view

2. Right intention

Ethical Conduct

3. Right speech

4. Right action

5. Right livelihood

Mental Discipline

6. Right effort

7. Right mindfulness

8. Right concentration

Our life—or lives, because we believe one can have many lives—is a continual turning of a wheel. Our illusions and sufferings do not end until we can see the reality of things. We call this wheel of suffering "samsara." We keep suffering until we get off the wheel. However, how can we get off of a wheel that we do not yet see? We will just keep running after things that keep fading as we try to grasp them. Therefore, we must do first things first: We must see the wheel. We must realize that the emperor has no clothes!

Didn't you just love Gary Larson's cartoons? (Does anyone know why he stopped drawing them?) His cartoons were always so wonderful. Anyway, in one of them, a carload of amoebas are rushing down a long winding road in this strange tunnellike place. One of the little amoebas in the back of the car says to the other one, "Wow, we're going on vacation to the large intestine!"

The little amoebas are so happy about going into the great intestine! Perhaps they are as happy as we are about shopping, getting a face-lift, or having a new and exciting romance. Turning, turning, turning; we're all on the wheel, whether we are amoebas or stockbrokers.

Bill Murray kept right on repeating Groundhog Day, changing the details ever so slightly, slowly, slowly discovering the wheel. Finally he simply rested in the delight of each fleeting moment. That's when the wheel stopped. (Go get that movie and laugh your way into becoming a Buddhist!)

When I came to believe that the four noble truths accurately described the world in which we live, I decided to "take refuge in the three jewels." What I mean by that is that I took refuge in Buddha, in the dharma (the teachings of Buddhism), and in the "sanga" (the community of Buddhists).

To take refuge in the Buddha is to acknowledge that no one out there is going to save me. I must discover my own Buddha nature, just as Siddhartha did so long ago.

To take refuge in the dharma is to diligently apply myself to learning the truth about the nature of reality, not primarily through the intellect but through the inner apprehension of the reality to which the teachings point.

To take refuge in the sanga is to realize that others have learned lessons from which I can profit. Others can coach me as I find my way through the illusions and self-deceptions that my mind is apt to put in my path.

Some Things Buddhism Offers the Modern Western World
We were asked to suggest what our faith offers the modern world. I came up with these:

- a worldview compatible with new discoveries in physics,

- techniques for brain and nervous system training, and

- inner peace.

Like Dr. Upadhyaya, I believe the Western world is facing a gigantic identity crisis. During the twentieth century, the paradigms of science, morality, and social structure were seriously challenged. The theories of relativity proposed by Albert Einstein proved to be accurate descriptions of the way the universe works. The quantum theories, also developed early in the century we have just concluded, described how matter behaves at the foundational levels of our world. The stuff from which atoms are made, as small to the atoms as the atoms are to us, exist only statistically and then only when we observe them! From the standpoint of traditional Western common sense, that is sheer madness.

As advances in physics and other sciences become known at the popular level, the cultural ground seemed to move beneath our feet. So we desperately need a new paradigm of knowledge that allows us to make a connection between these advances and our everyday lives.

It is truly amazing that Buddhists have felt all along that what we call reality consists of impermanent and constantly shifting patterns of energy and mind. Therefore, Buddhists are not at all troubled by the new discoveries of physics.

I also think that Buddhism offers much where brain and nervous system training are concerned. After all, questions about consciousness have preoccupied Buddhists for centuries.

I teach a course on William James at California State, and I try to get my psychology students to read his *Principles of Psychology*. Until recently, James's ideas about neurology were thought to be terribly outdated. However, I have discovered that when my students really wrestle with James's thoughts, they begin making new discoveries. They often develop new kinds of therapy to help people as well.

James was an early theorist in the field of psychology. I think Americans ignored him because they became too enthralled with European thinkers like Freud. That's beside the point though. The important thing to note about James is that he came up with several theories about the brain and nervous system that seem close indeed to what Buddhists have traditionally taught. James didn't have the ability to test his theories because medical research on the brain was so primitive. Lately, though, several discoveries in the field of neurology have proven that he was generally correct.

Over a century ago, William James speculated that events, relationships, and other kinds of experience probably impacted our physical brain structures. He used the allegory of rain falling on a hillside. The rain creates little rivulets. Rain that falls after the rivulets have formed will tend to follow those same paths already cut into the earth. In the same way, James figured, brains may tend to be most receptive to those ideas and experiences that match the patterns already established within its mental structure. However, just as it is possible to cut a new path into the hillside so that water from future rains will take a different course, people can create new neuro-pathways and connections within their brains. That will seriously alter the way they will experience future opportunities or challenges.

Trauma can do this, of course. Education can do it too. So can spiritual enlightenment.

Jeffrey Swartz, in his book *The Mind and the Brain,* uses these ideas about "neuroplasicity" (a word that refers to the brain's ability to train itself and to regenerate at the cellular level) to address the problem

the end of suffering

of obsessive-compulsive behavior. He suggests techniques very similar to those Buddhists might use to bring order to their thoughts and emotions.

Buddhists believe that we can bring an end to our suffering simply by turning away from the craving that creates the suffering. Many neurologists are coming to similar conclusions.

Years ago I saw a cartoon in some old magazine. (I think it was *Omni* magazine—does anyone remember *Omni?* Gosh, it was great.) In this cartoon, two aliens are crossing a desert on some faraway planet. They are obviously about to give out. One of them has a tentacle stretched out as far as it will go and is moaning, "Ammonia! Ammonia! My kingdom for one drop of ammonia!"

Torri laughed again, and once again the entire group laughed with her.

Isn't it interesting that although *what* we crave may differ considerably from culture to culture and from person to person, the fact *that* we crave is always the source of our pain?

This being so, doesn't it make sense that we would work to turn away from the world of illusions and craving and return to the reality of our true nature?

Nichiren Daishonin wrote in the thirteenth century about this. He taught that we can begin our journey toward wholeness by simply chanting, "Nam myoho renge kyo" with our whole heart. This is the invocation of the Lotus Sutra. It shows us the way to turn from suffering and toward that compassion of heart that finally engulfs all sentient beings.

I thank you, my dear new friends, for your kindness and for all you may teach me in these important discussions. It is my hope that I may have offered some light for your journey as I'm sure you will do for mine.

With these words, Torri folded her hands together and extended them like a steeple for a moment just under her chin. She was motionless for a few seconds and then asked for questions.

JOURNAL NOTES

One of the most difficult shifts that individual Western Christians will have to make in our postmodern, globalized, technologically advanced century is to relate in their day-to-day lives with people of other religions. Christians in India and the Middle East have had long experience with this. Christians in the West have not. Until quite recently, few Hindus or Muslims lived in most of our American towns and cities. Now this has changed.

Christians are going to discover that people of other religions are not usually sinister or frightening. Many times they will be like Torri Adams. She is a delightful human being. She is intelligent, warm, and full of life. Most people experience her as an extremely interesting person. It is difficult to resist her compelling presentation of Buddhism.

Torri is all of these things because Buddhism is all these things! It is an extremely interesting system of thought. It appeals to one's intellect. It offers a practice that appeals to one's emotions. If offers a community of kind people where one can find immediate acceptance.

What does a Christian do with this reality?

When I first began to read Buddhist material, I became confused. I even wondered how it could even be called a religion. Of course, if the first Buddhist that a Christian encounters is a Tibetan, the mystical otherworldliness of that particular perspective will probably cause some alarm. We expect to encounter weirdness and spooky practices in other religions. But that otherworldy kind of Buddhism is very much the exception! Torri's version is more the norm.

If Christians encounter Zen or the various kinds of Theravada practice, they will probably be surprised that the deities, rites, and sacred practices they expected to find will be completely absent. In fact, Christians are amazed to find out that in Zen, an attachment to holy things (including devotion to the Buddha) are viewed as likely impediments to one's spiritual growth.

Many schools of Buddhism will strike the Christian as more like Eastern forms of humanism than like religion as we customarily think of it. (That is assuming of course that humanism is not a religion—but that is another subject.) Buddhists do not believe in a personal creator. That makes perfect sense because they also do not believe in the personhood of human beings, at least as a Westerner defines a person.

Buddhism as Psychology

Buddhist practice is focused largely upon identifying, monitoring, and expanding one's internal state of consciousness. Does that allow us to view

Buddhism as much as a psychology as a religion? If so, can we not appreciate the centuries of observation, reflection, and practical applications relating to mental health that Buddhist scholars have developed? And if we respect this work, can we not learn from it?

These are the sorts of questions that Christians will increasingly face as Western studies of human consciousness continue to become ever more respectable.

Until recently, Western speculation on the nature of consciousness took place among philosophers. The phenomenologists were particularly interested in developing dependable means for self-observation. Literary figures, such as Dostoyevsky, also were interested in the subject.

Early psychologists were interested for a while—William James wrote extensively about consciousness—but their findings were largely discarded by a field trying to establish itself as a respectable science. Most scientists believed that the speculation on the nature of consciousness would come to little until they could lead to verifiable theories about materially observable phenomena within the brain.

Western science has been mystified for a long time about the core human experience—the sense that we are inside our own selves, observing a world that is outside our heads. Science was supposed to deal with objects. However, thoughts are not objects; they cannot be observed by anyone except the one who thinks them. How then could mental processes become an authentic part of scientific research?

The development of new medical technology began to change the nature of consciousness studies. The EEG, PET, and MRI devices enabled researchers to peer into the mysterious workings of living human brains. Neurology began to expand its field to include studies in the nature of consciousness. Researchers could observe and record the differences in states of consciousness—dreams, trances, trauma, anxiety, and various stages of meditation.

As neurologists and psychologists expanded their inquiry into the workings of the human mind, they naturally became interested in the work of earlier theorists. Edmund Husserl and other phenomenologists had developed helpful theories about how to link one's observations of his or her own thoughts with the images of the thinker's brain being observed by scientists.

As in so many other fields, neurology was forced to reconsider Western science's long disdain for subjective speculation. Some of the Western world's intellectual giants had already begun to observe the workings of the human mind from the inside. Such speculation was filled with traps, to be sure. However, people like William James and Edmund Husserl proved that the attempt was worth the effort.

It was only a matter of time before some of the more adventuresome scientists would discover the Eastern tradition of consciousness studies. Once Western thinkers like Francisco Valera began to meet with the Dali Lama, the stage was set for a growing dialogue between Buddhists and Western neurologists. That dialogue has seriously influenced the course of theory and therapy among American mental health practitioners.

The influence of Buddhism on the mental health field has thus been subtle, but it has been persistent. It has, for the most part, also been beneficial.

What does a Christian say about that? Should a Christian regard Buddhist influence on psychology as more dangerous to our faith than the old materialistic (and often antireligious) paradigm that ruled the mental health field from Freud until fairly recently? If so, why?

My own encounters with Buddhism have been pleasant, like the one I experienced with Torri. If I view Buddhism as an ancient Eastern approach to psychology and philosophy, I cease being resentful of its new Western influence. I began to understand its intellectual and emotional allure. I may even view it as an ally in our struggle against militant secularism.

Christians have always found ways to utilize the insights of others, even if in reaction against those insights. The church fathers accepted the Jewish counsel of Jamnia's decision (AD 90) about the Old Testament canon. St. Thomas Aquinas consulted Islam's Avicenna and Judaism's Maimonides as he wrote his theological masterpiece. For that matter, megachurch pastors have no problem using the insights of Madison Avenue and Wall Street, institutions not noted for their piety or theological orthodoxy.

That modern Christians tend to feel less threatened by secular influences than religious ones is a curious phenomenon. Perhaps it is because secular forces seem neutral and therefore less dangerous. But is that a reasonable opinion? Is the Buddha really more of a danger to our faith than Hugh Hefner or Donald Trump?

Buddhism as a Means of Personal Training

I can go further with this train of thought. I can affirm that many of the Buddha's insights agree with those of our own Scripture. Like the Buddha, we too believe in "dukkha," the fact that our lives have an out-of-sortness

the end of suffering

to them. Something doesn't seem right about the world because something is not right about the world.

Christians also believe in "tanha," or as medieval Christian writers expressed it, "inordinate desire." It is what the Bible means by "lust," a word that our modern world has reduced to refer merely to sexual desire. Lust in the older sense is very close to what the Buddha described as a fire that feeds upon our constant grasping for illusions.

As for the eightfold path: How these ideas resonate with the book of Proverbs! And the Psalmist describes a life of submission to God in a way that might make a Buddhist on the eightfold path seem very much like a fellow traveler.

Why Buddhism and Christianity are Incompatible

I remember when I first heard the "Buddhist creed," or the "Three Refuges":

> I take refuge in the Buddha.
> I take refuge in the dharma (teachings).
> I take refuge in the sanga (community).

I was moved by the confession. I even wrote it down so I could reflect upon it in depth. For many months afterward, I found myself praying this:

> I take refuge in Jesus.
> I take refuge in the Holy Scripture.
> I take refuge in the body of Christ.

This was where I began to uncover the great distance that separates Buddhism from Christianity. When a Buddhist claims to take refuge in the Buddha, he means something very different from what I mean by taking refuge in the Christ. Buddhists view the founder of their faith as a model of enlightenment. They honor him as a great teacher. Nothing prohibits a Christian from viewing the Buddha in this way too. However, when Christians take refuge in the Christ, they are doing much more than showing respect to a great teacher. Christians take refuge in Jesus because Jesus is the Savior of their souls.

Another point of agreement with Buddhism is the notion that our minds need to be changed. The New Testament Greek word that we usually translate as "repentance" is "metanoia" (to change one's mind). Like the Buddha, St. Paul urges us to carefully choose what we will think about.

Whatever things are true, whatever things are noble, whatever things are just, whatever things are pure, whatever things are lovely, whatever things are of good report, if there is any virtue and if there is anything praiseworthy—meditate on these things.[1]

In another place, Paul tells us, "Do not be conformed to this world, but be transformed by the renewing of your mind."[2]

Even converted men and women must constantly make decisions about how and where to focus their minds. Here again we can find substantial agreement with Buddhism.

However, something more wonderfully intimate and holy is intended than mere mental focus when a Christian sings, "Jesus, Lover of my soul / Let me to thy bosom fly."[3]

Jesus, Scripture, and the Church

I take refuge in Jesus because I believe Him to be very God of very God, wholly God and wholly man. I believe He was begotten (not created) before all worlds. He is light of light, the expressed image of the invisible God, the Word made flesh, light of the Gentiles, and soon to be crowned Lord of the universe.

I take refuge in Jesus because He—for us sinners—was made flesh and became a man. He suffered under Pontius Pilate, died, was buried, and rose again the third day.

That is real refuge! It is what was meant by the old gospel song, "I've anchored my soul in the haven of rest," and especially in the last line of the song, "In Jesus I'm safe evermore." [4] In contrast, a Buddhist does not believe we need a savior; only a teacher.

I also take refuge in the Holy Scriptures. Life has taught me that I need "a lamp to my feet and light to my path."[5] I have discovered that the Word of God gives joy to the heart and makes wise the simple.

Taking refuge in the Scripture does not mean that I become blind and deaf to the discoveries of science or hostile to social change. I don't undermine the Scripture by making claims for the Bible that it does not make for itself. However, taking refuge in the Scripture means that I resist the tendency to devalue its authority or to subvert its clear moral messages.

The stories of the Scripture were my delight in childhood; its doctrines became my intellectual trainer as an adult. Its prayers are becoming my solace as I age. I take refuge in this book because I believe it to be the voice of God in a printed form. It is a literary incarnation of God. I open its pages and converse with my Creator.

Finally, I take refuge in the community of Jesus—the church. That's harder for me. My greatest sorrows have come from my disillusionments with the church. Churches have often tempted me to organize my life around fear and suspicion. They have sometimes offered me ignorance dressed up as piety. They have sometimes led me to believe that no one could possibly be both an adult male and a holy man! And yet, in spite of all of this, I take refuge in the church.

Why?

I suppose I feel toward the church what Peter expressed toward Jesus when the Lord asked him if he intended go away. "Lord," the apostle replied, "to whom shall we go? You have the words of eternal life."[6]

The church is terribly flawed and often much too human. If a believer doesn't keep this in mind, sooner or later the church will break his heart. On the other hand, I have experienced times in which the church suddenly becomes much more than the sum of its parts, times when the Spirit moves through the church to heal, deliver, and transform the world. I take refuge in that.

The church is the body of Christ, "the pillar and ground of the truth."[7] She is in need of constant reformation and loving confrontation, but the church is the community of Jesus, and I take refuge in that community.

Many years ago, in a large city in China, I realized that it was Sunday morning. I began to walk the streets, trying to find a church. I finally found a building with a simple, small cross on the door. As I stood looking at the cross, a man asked me in very poor English if I wanted to go inside. When I told him that I did, he motioned for me to wait. Soon he returned with an old lady who was carrying some keys.

A couple of my friends had arrived by this time, and one of them could speak Chinese.

When we stepped inside the building, I saw that it was nearly empty. There were a few chairs and an old Sunday school depiction of Christ with the children on the back wall.

The woman told me that this was a Catholic church. She asked if we were believers, and when she discovered we were, she apologized because there would be no service that day. The priest would be there the following Sunday, she explained.

When she told us that she had been in jail because of her faith, we were moved. When she saw our tears, she asked us to pray.

As we were leaving, she said, "We will not meet again here. We will meet in the Spirit when we pray. Then, soon, we will all be together forever."

As I left, I felt that I was leaving a part of myself.

That is what gives me refuge in a fallen world.

I think a Buddhist would see this as an attachment or clinging, as something that causes pain. I view the pain as a form of love. If that is attachment, so be it.

God Our Savior

I have a more fundamental reason for insisting that Buddhism and Christianity are wholly incomparable. It is one of the most obvious differences one can imagine: I believe in God.

That is the first line of both of Christianity's central creeds. It is based on the very first verse of the first book of the Bible. It is a constant theme in all we say and do.

This is not true of Buddhism. Buddhists do not say, "I believe in God, the Father Almighty."

Our Scripture tells us that "it is He who has made us, and not we ourselves."[8] Therefore, we cannot be self-created illusions, as Buddhists insist. A "self" cannot be regarded as spiritual pathology if a personal God has made us to be real persons.

Christianity believes that we are "selves" and that the one who created us is a self. God is a person, or to be more theologically accurate, three persons. Furthermore, this self who created us seeks to evoke our full potential as selves. In other words, God is not wooing us toward a final extinction in which we lose all identity and differentiation from the Godhead.

God then, is a self who seeks to relate to other selves. He desires that His children grow to full stature. Relationship thus requires distinction as well as union. Therefore, spiritual maturity involves both individualization and interdependence.

Our relationship with God is not merely one between a teacher and pupils. It is one between a Savior and sinners. For I am not only ignorant, I am lost. To use a good Buddhist word, life is "dukkha." We are bent, out of sorts, twisted, and broken. We need more than a teacher, even a great teacher like the Buddha.

We need a Savior.

Our Savior must have compassion on us. Buddhists tell us that Shakyamuni had compassion, and we have no reason to dispute them. However, our Savior must not only have compassion for us as we are, He must have sufficient power to transform us into what we should be.

Even great training cannot transform us if we are bent and broken. One of the central teachings of the New Testament is in fact that we are too broken to keep rules, even if they are God's rules. Even Torah—God's law—can't save us. So although we must be trained in godliness, training will not make us godly because "all have sinned and fall short."[9]

That is why Christ, the Teacher, became a sacrifice and a Savior. The Apostles' Creed affirms that He now "sits at the right hand of God, the Father Almighty." Christians believe without such supernatural help, we lack the power to transform ourselves.

We also need ongoing help and guidance. That's why we confess, in the words of the Nicene Creed, that "we believe in the Holy Spirit, the Lord and giver of life."

The Holy Spirit lives in believers, strengthening their will and thereby helping them to choose the ways of God.

A Christian believes that God is our heavenly Father. He created us and seeks our salvation, even before we ever submit to Him.

God is also our human Friend, our Teacher, who became one of us in our joys and sorrows.

Finally, God is an abiding presence within our very being, strengthening our growth in goodness and grace and directing us toward our final transformation.

Thus, we are covered, surrounded, and saturated with God as we study and apply the teachings of Holy Scripture to our lives in the company of other believers.

A few Buddhist sects, such as the one to which Torri Adams belongs, use similar language as that of Christians when describing their spiritual journey. Like us, the so-called Pure Land Buddhists also depend upon the boundless merit of a savior. The difference between them and Christians, however, is much greater than the similar language would suggest. The difference lies in the meaning that each religion assigns to the meaning of "Savior" and "salvation."

The Pure Land Buddhists, like all other Buddhists, seek deliverance from their own sense of being and personhood. They see no alternative to the grasping, lusting self, with all the resulting suffering and sorrow, except to eliminate self through an experience of enlightenment that destroys the illusion of personhood.

In contrast, Christians seek salvation from the disease that destroys self. To a Christian, the alternative to a diseased self is not "no self," as Buddhists believe, but a redeemed self.

We believe that relationship with God and with other humans requires a distinction as well as a union. Indeed, we believe that within God Himself are distinctions as well as unity. God as Creator is distinguished from God as Redeemer and from God who is our Comforter. Yet these distinctions neither divide the unity nor eliminate the differences.

This principle—of difference and distinction within unity—is a foundational belief of Christian theology and Christian spirituality. It is what enables us to view marriage as a unity of selves rather than as a relationship in which one self gradually consumes the other. It also allows us to experience our various denominations within Christianity as temporary and trivial distinctions within the unbroken body of Christ.

Buddhists can say much that is wise, helpful, and consistent with our own view of life and goodness. However, Buddhism's failure to acknowledge the Creator as a personal being who loves us and seeks to know us is, we believe, a fundamental error. Furthermore, viewing salvation as a flight from personhood and a journey toward an eventual extinguishing of self seems to deny that we are made in the image and likeness of God.

For all these reasons, we must part company with the great teacher of the East, even while honoring his life, his words, and his legacy. He was a great human being, one of the greatest. But he cannot save us.

Salvation is our greatest need, so we must seek a path and a person that promises us deliverance from our sin as well as deliverance from our ignorance and our illusions.

at one with the earth:
the native american way

*The soil you see is not ordinary soil—it is the dust of
the blood, the flesh and the bones of our ancestors. The
land as it is, is my blood and dead; it is consecrated
and I do not want to give up any portion of it.*

CROW DECLARATION TO THE UNITED STATES GOVERNMENT

Francisco Puma was born in the small village of Yaruquies, several
kilometers southwest of Riobamba, Ecuador. In the early years of
Francisco's schooling, a Peace Corps worker took notice of his exceptional
intelligence and talked about him to a wealthy woman in Riobamba. That
woman, Señora Rosa Maria Cardozo de Jimenez, decided to sponsor Francisco's education.

Señora de Jimenez followed the progress of the young student as he made
his way through various grades. Later, she fought to place him in a prestigious boarding school in Quito, called El Collegio de San Juan de la Cruz.
She faced considerable social resistance to the idea of placing a Quechua-speaking boy in the school where children from established families like
hers had attended for nearly three hundred years. She persevered, however.
That's where Francisco later applied for a scholarship to the University of
South Dakota, in their Native American studies program.

A retired missionary had established the scholarship program at the University of South Dakota in the 1930s. He had specified that the scholarship
was for indigenous South Americans who desired to study native cultures.
The program for which it provided funds would be connected to the school
of anthropology. Through the years, the school had encountered difficulty
locating students who could qualify for this scholarship. In fact, no one had
even applied in several years.

Jeffries Blanchett, a graduate of the University of South Dakota, was teaching English at El Collegio de San Juan de la Cruz in 1984, the year Francisco Puma became a sophomore. He quickly realized that Francisco was a young man of considerable abilities. So Jeffries thought of his young student when he read the short announcement from the school of anthropology in his alumni quarterly. He contacted the department head, met with Señora de Jimenez to get funds for a trip to America, and told Francisco about the opportunity.

The year after Francisco's summer trip to South Dakota, Jeffries worked to improve the young man's English. He also stressed the importance of remaining connected to his native language and to the people in Yaruquies. After all, the Native American studies program was intended to help students gain a wide perspective of indigenous cultures of the Americas. Francisco would not only be studying such cultures, he would be representing one.

Jeffries led Francisco to develop pride in Quechua, which had been the language of the Inca empire. The people who still spoke it were the remnants of a powerful people who had ruled and cultivated a vast area. The Incas had built cities in the mountains that still baffle engineers. Jeffries urged Francisco to stop trying to ignore his own roots, to stop trying to force his way into a culture that would never fully accept him. The program in South Dakota was an opportunity to do that.

Francisco Puma did well in the University of South Dakota. In fact, he went on to study anthropology in graduate school, finally receiving his doctorate from the University of Oklahoma. He had become a respected advocate for Native American culture and had spoken twice before delegates of the United Nations. He had been working for a year with the University of Arizona when he received Glen's invitation to speak at our interfaith conference.

He showed up to our meeting wearing a pair of simple white cotton pants that ended halfway between his knees and his ankles. His belt was a thin rope, and his shoes were the quilted-rope sandals that Andean natives often wear. He wore a black hat with a green cord around its brim, and he had black shoulder-length hair. He wore a white pullover short-sleeve cotton shirt and a leather cord around his neck, upon which was some sort of talon or claw.

His English was clear and easily understood, with a Spanish accent that was not like most I had heard. He pronounced "sh" and "ch" very strongly and sometimes placed an aspirated sound before words that began with a vowel. It was a pleasant accent though, and it made his obvious learning more compelling.

He jumped right into his topic.

It is a sign of progress that I have been invited here to speak to you about Native American religion. Even in the recent past, the indigenous spiritual and religious perspectives of the Americas were dismissed as primitive, of little significance for serious study. This has been the prevailing academic attitude toward the spiritual practices of Native peoples in the Americas until very recently. I am therefore grateful for the progress we have made. For this reason, I hesitate to begin my remarks with this negative comment: There really is no such thing as a Native American religion.

The various indigenous peoples of the Americas have differed from one another in culture and religious practices as much as Jews, Christians, and Muslims have differed from one another. To an outsider, these three faiths appear amazingly similar, but they do not seem similar to those who practice them.

Jews, Christians, and Muslims all worship one supreme Creator God. All three believe that this one God has sent prophets with commandments by which humanity is expected to live. All three religions tell us that the holy books these prophets have written must be read, studied, and obeyed. All three religions teach that those who submit to the one God should assemble with others who submit to God in order to create communities. God's will is proclaimed and put into practice through these communities. Understandably then, these similarities strike an outsider as much more important than the differences.

I realize that what I have just said may offend the people of all three groups. I also realize that the differences between these Abrahamic religions are extremely important to those who follow them.

I make this comparison simply to help us understand what is gained and what is lost by using a term like "Native American religion." On one hand, the term allows us explore ideas that are common to the peoples of the Americas. On the other hand, such a broad term encourages us to overlook the unique insights of each of the various peoples who live on our two great American continents. These unique treasures are rapidly becoming extinct. Soon they may be lost forever. So my concern is not about making a politically correct statement; it is about expressing a historical, social, and spiritual reality.

at one with the earth

I know by experience that many people think it poor taste to dwell on the tragic loss of Native America. Nearly every nation in the Americas continued the policies of genocide and dislocation that the colonizing European powers began. What disease and pillage did not accomplish, state-sponsored murder did. Thus we have lost many languages, medicines, arts, and religions that could have made major contributions to our understanding of human life on our planet. No one in this room is to blame for this. Therefore, little purpose is served by angry rhetoric. Nonetheless, it is important for us to look at the religions of the Native peoples through this tragic historical reality. This rape of Native America was, like slavery, perpetrated by a Christian people who claimed to stand on high moral ground.

This was true of the Spanish, the French, the Portuguese, the English, and the Dutch. It was true of Catholics, Protestants, and the Russian Orthodox. Each of the European powers used religion and commerce as ways to dismantle, assimilate, remove, and redefine the religions, social order, art, languages, and customs of the people who had lived in the Americas for thousands of years before the great wave of undocumented immigrants began to arrive from Europe. We may say then that Christianity was the moral justification for the rape of the Americas, although the priests, pastors, and missionaries were often not deliberately compliant with this strategy of cultural genocide.

I mention Christianity specifically because it became the spiritual competitor of Native culture. Its victory in this competition has been so overwhelming that it is now difficult to discern what once belonged to the original Native culture and what has been borrowed or created as a reaction to the faith of our colonizers.

I do not mean my remarks as an attack on contemporary Christians, of course. Many Natives are very fervent Christians after all. Also, I am not unaware of the sincere help that some Christian groups offer Native peoples; in fact, I have been a recipient of such help. What I want to establish is simply that the Native American culture that managed to survive, did so despite all efforts to eliminate it. Moreover, even in their survival, the Native cultures have been deeply influenced by their long struggle with European and Christian values.

Today I will try to describe those religious values to which most Native peoples relate.

Let's begin with an insight from Ake Hultkrantz. We can divide

Native religious perspectives into two broad categories: those with roots in a hunting culture and those with roots in a farming culture. Those with hunting roots tended toward shamanism, and those with roots in farming tended toward ritualized reenactments of their tribal mythology.

Let me try to explain what Hultkrantz meant by this.

Take Christianity, for example. In the Episcopal church, where I attended a few times in South Dakota, the worship calendar revolves around seasonal change. Walking through the year together and participating in the familiar dramas of sacramental action unite people to one another and the living to the dead. This is an example of a religion based on agriculture. (There is a reason that Episcopalians call their long summer stretch "ordinary time" and mark the season with the color green! There is not much to do but hoe and wait in the summer, when the things one planted in the spring are now busy growing.)

The leader of a church based on agriculture is expected to have wisdom, patience, and forbearance because he (and increasingly, she) represents a planted and stable culture.

At the other end of the Christian spectrum, consider the Pentecostals. This form of Christianity operates without reference to the seasons or even to connections with the past. Pentecostals expect that something spiritually significant should happen each time they meet. Therefore, the leader of a Pentecostal church (as Harvey Cox has pointed out) should be more like a shaman. That is to say that the leader should be able to access an altered state in which he or she connects the worshippers to supernatural power. This is indicative of those religious expressions Hultkrantz believed were based on a hunting culture.

I did a summer program once at Escota, North Carolina. While there, I attended snake-handling services several times and was fascinated by trance-inducing actions and speech of the worshippers. The snake handlers are extreme examples of shamanistic forms of Christianity and illustrate the way we can categorize Native American religion.

It is probably more than a coincidence that what Americans now call Appalachia was once called the Cherokee Nation! Before it was destroyed, the Cherokee people had intermarried extensively with European settlers. In fact, a few decades after the American Revolution, most of the Cherokee had become Christians. Of course, their conversion did not keep President Jackson from having them forcibly removed after settlers discovered gold on Cherokee land. By that time, however, many Cherokees had become so interconnected with European families that it had become impossible to remove all of the original culture or the native bloodline from the land. Therefore, the practices of some Christian sects in the area were influenced by Native spirituality.

The movements in American history called the Great Awakenings were marked by phenomena previously unknown to European Christians. The use of dance to induce altered states of consciousness, story-telling as a way to induce communal trance, and even the unique mountain melodies of groups indigenous to Appalachia reflect their Native roots. This point can be stressed too heavily of course, but it helps European people view Native spirituality as something a little less foreign and exotic.

More to my point, the agriculturally based cultures in the Americas produced religious expressions that were rich in myth and cosmological speculation. The Hopi are an example of this. Hopi religious thought is complex and highly structured, and it offers a view of the world as strikingly unique as that of any world religion.

Surprisingly, though, the more shamanistic expressions of Native spirituality now seem to have the greatest appeal for modern Americans. Therefore, many of my remarks today will revolve around the worldview, practice, and effects of shamanism. Just realize that shamanistic practices of Native peoples are often displayed in caricature for the benefit of tourists. They are also exploited in film and print for uses far removed from their original context.

In fact, the very word "shaman" is a term more accurately used for spiritual leaders in Asia than in the Americas. However, its popular meaning has become so much broader than that, so I reluctantly use it today to refer to certain types of Native American spiritual leaders.

I won't even take the time to dignify the likes of Carlos Castaneda and others who deliberately exploit falsified accounts of Native spirituality. Native American religion is, in some ways, a screen upon which many people project their own inventions and illusions. We want to avoid this if at all possible.

Reverence Toward the Earth

It can be difficult to talk about Native spirituality without falling into the stereotypes created by Europeans. This is because the Natives themselves have often accepted the stereotypes and used them to their own economic advantage. If tourists wanted feathers on our heads, we gave them some feathers! Whether our particular tribe ever used feathers became irrelevant. If some rich white people wanted to get intoxicated on peyote, they could usually find some entrepreneurial Indian to shake a gourd while the white men fried their brains!

Many people in the Americas are now looking in the Native cultures for things of worth they believe have been lost by the culture as a whole. The lines between fantasy and fact—between wishful thinking and careful research—are now routinely ignored by otherwise intelligent people. Their spiritual curiosity has become so strong that they use the Native cultures, particularly those of the past, as screens upon which to project their own internal needs of an intimate connection with the universe.

People who want to make a little money can always find ways to help people produce a more powerful fantasy!

A few years ago, a man who lived in Puyo, Ecuador—a town that in those days was where the road ended and the jungle began—would visit the hotels and tell tourists about a "reluctant" Indian medicine man in the forest who performed astounding cures and spells. Every month, some of the tourists would pay him a few dollars so he would persuade the medicine man to allow them to observe his magic. They would go to a cave, where they would get nearly naked and watch a guy covered with animal skins do sleight-of-hand tricks with pieces of bloody meat that he claimed were diseased parts of their internal organs. The scam made the guys a decent living until the department of tourism made them stop.

This sort of thing happens all over the world wherever people from industrial countries search for the missing parts of their soul. Fraud is often easy to perpetrate when people become hungry for transcendent experience.

But I would like for us to remember that like most caricatures, the exaggerated and sometimes even false Native American symbols and ceremonies are usually based on elements of fact. The man in Puyo who was making money creating false ceremonies for tourists had actually witnessed such ceremonies deep in the jungle.

The modern caricatures of Native beliefs, though often distorted by Europeans and even by other Natives for political and economic reasons, are usually connected to deeply held ideas about how the world works. For example, most Native cultures do indeed reverence the earth and believe it is possible to communicate with the spirits of animals, plants, and other elements of nature.

My grandfather, Taita Ramón, was a devout Roman Catholic, but he would nonetheless begin the work of planting corn by mumbling a kind of chant:

> *Sara, sara*
> *Mushuc sara*
> *Huasicunaman*

He would say this at each row, inviting the corn spirit to come into our fields and make its home with us. The following day, he would have the priest come and sprinkle holy water on the land. Taita Ramón wanted to keep all his bases covered!

Most people in Native cultures speak to nature in this intimate way. Hunters talk to the spirits of the animals they will kill, asking permission to partake of their life force. The farmers, like my grandfather, talk to the spirits of the plants. All people in ancient times depended on the goodwill of the natural environment. They had to have an abundance of crops or animals in order to live. Therefore, they naturally tended to have a sense of reverence and respect for these sources of life.

Most of the peoples of the Americas did not think of any part of the natural order as "inanimate," which is why I have tried to avoid the word in this discussion. Waterfalls, mountains, and canyons were thought to be embodiments of wisdom or power. These places may speak to a person; they may even feel like the womb from which a people believe they emerged, or the breasts that gave them nurture and strength.

We have many volcanoes in our country. Two of them are near where I was raised and are very active. They are called Tungurahua (Throat of Fire) and Sangay. When we talk about them, we say their names respectfully. Most Native peoples have this kind of affection and respect for the important places around them.

Today, in South and Central America, places of spiritual importance will usually be marked by Christian shrines to saints. Often, however, these shrines are built from the ruins of indigenous shrines from the pre-Christian era. So this sense of place and communication with the natural environment is extremely important.

These features of Native culture imply that an environmental aware-ness is a vital part of our lives. This feature of Native life is often used by environmentalists as a source for their ethics and assumptions. They are essentially correct in these assumptions, but we should remember that Native peoples also harmed their environment, although not intention-ally and certainly not on any massive scale as people can do today. The Aztecs and Mayans, for example, essentially destroyed their immediate environments; they did not understand the natural limits to sustainability of human culture within a rain forest. (Modern Brazil, which has access to all the facts about these limits, nonetheless aggressively pushes its plans to create new massive cities in the middle of the Amazon jungle.)

Despite the few examples of overbuilding in environments that could not sustain urban centers, Native Americans organized their social lives in ways that were respectful of their surroundings. So envi-ronmentalists are correct in basing their views on Native beliefs about how human life should honor the natural order that sustains it.

This respect for the natural order was not unique to the Americas. The same kinds of attitudes were found all around the world until fairly recently. Native American leaders are increasingly making connections with other indigenous peoples, especially in Asia and Polynesia. As they do, we learn that other indigenous people have similar ways of relating to nature. They face similar struggles as they try to survive the aggres-sive march of global industrialization.

The indigenous cultures often contain vast knowledge, gleaned over millennia, about the medicinal use of plants and minerals and what these natural ingredients can do to affect human consciousness. Aspirin came from Native medicine. So did quinine. Respect for these cultures with their enduring links to the dawn of human history may well save life on this planet. Much evil has already been done to the traditional cultures of the world. We cannot undo that damage, and bitterness does not empower anyone. But we can resolve to honor what remains and try to reconstruct what has been lost. In this way, we will be preserving for all time the culture of a people who once lived here and did all they knew to do to honor the land with gratitude and reverence.

Dreams, Visions, and Trances

Native American societies had no scripture. Their mythology, theologi-cal formation, and liturgical traditions were almost entirely oral. There were some exceptions, such as the famous Aztec calendars carved on stone, but in general, Native Americans had no recorded text. How then could they consult the sacred powers of their lives for wisdom and guidance?

We have already talked about how nature itself was rather like a book to be discerned, debated, and honored. However, the messages of nature were not always understood. The signs sometimes seemed to give contradictory words. Therefore, most Native cultures relied on dreams and visions.

Sometimes communication from the spirit world came unsought. Spirits of animals and plants would speak to the people in dreams at night, telling them where to hunt or to plant their crops. At other times, the spirits did not come to human beings, so human beings had to design ways to go into the world of the spirits.

When a group of Native peoples needed a message from the spiritual world, they would approach a gifted and trained person who knew how to enter trance through the use of certain foods, herbs, dance, sleep deprivation, or other sorts of ritual action. Entering trance in this way was not thought of as a way to entertain irrationality, as Europeans believed. A dream state was not unreality but rather another part of reality. If a wolf came in a dream or drug-induced trance, the person was supposed to follow the wolf and experience what the wolf wished to reveal. Upon waking from the dream or trance, the man or woman who had talked with the wolf would decide what actions were required to honor what he or she had experienced.

Ironically, the Native reliance on dreams and visions opened the doors for several Christian groups who came to spread their faith. One missionary group from Russia reported that when they arrived at what is now Alaska, the Native peoples were already waiting for them with food and warm clothes! They discovered that the shaman had seen them coming in a trance and had been told by the spirits that the strangers from the West would be bringing important words on animal skins.

Christians tell stories like these, and they are probably based on real events. However, the dreams and visions sometimes instructed Native people to flee from the strangers. Whether to accommodate or to repel the peoples from Europe and Asia, Native men and women were often warned in advance of their coming by dreams and visions. This is a matter of historical record, often told by the invaders themselves.

Dreams and visions were particularly helpful for healing the illnesses of body, mind, or community.

Healing and Health

When Native Americans on this continent first began to speak English, they would often refer to their various kinds of healers as "medicine men." To a European, the word "medicine" has to do with pills and injections, so in this context, "medicine" is a substance. However, the Native peoples used the word in a much broader sense, as when we say that a person "practices medicine." We mean that such a person has knowledge about how to heal people.

"Medicine" in the Native American context is an intention to restore a person or a community to balance and wholeness. So a Native healer may perform a ceremony of some sort to restore harmony among a people who have been in conflict. The healer may ask a sick man or woman to observe a time of solitude and silence. The sick person may be asked to eat some herbs or to go on a very long walk. The idea in all of these actions is to provoke new insight into causes of distress, to encourage a breakthrough from some rut and routine, or to simply get a person moving in a new direction.

Medicine is about restoring health to the whole person. This means that healing can begin almost anywhere in that person's system: in the body, mind, spirit, or community. Once health is restored to one part of the person's life, it can spread to the other parts. Native medicine seeks to strengthen the entire system of life.

Some objects and locations are thought to be especially powerful containers of health, or medicine. Naturally, these objects or locations were held in high regard. In Quechua, such things are called "huacas." Although the Spanish translated the "huacas" to mean holy, the word "medicine" works much better in some contexts.

On the other hand, even in European languages, the words "holy," "whole," and "healthy" all derive from a common root. Doesn't the word "holy" mean that something, some person, or some event is somehow connected to that which is "whole," or unbroken? Christian theology views the world as broken or ill, so holy things, in contrast, are "whole" or "holy." So the Native idea is not as alien to European thought as it might first appear.

I would argue that in past ages Christian beliefs about healing and health were not as far apart from Native American notions as they are today. Modern European culture divided the individual's world into separate parts, each part becoming ever more disconnected from the others. A sick body became the concern of a person designated by the culture to deal only with physical bodies. A doctor then ceased to think about the sick person's family life or ask whether the patient felt connected to his or her occupation.

Western medicine kept dividing the individual up this way. Now a sick stomach requires a stomach specialist. A bad heart must be cared for by a cardiologist. If a patient has both a bad stomach and a bad heart, he sees two doctors who may not even know one another! Neither of the doctors will probably be concerned that the sick person has just gone through a divorce.

In contrast, when our town was facing some epidemic, the priest used to call a special mass. The doctors would not begin their work until the people had confessed their sins and participated in Holy Communion. Usually, the doctors would receive Communion with us. We would watch the priest bless them for the work they were about to do. This is medicine in the broad sense—restoring wholeness by paying attention to the whole.

When compared to Native American approaches to healing, however, even European religion failed to address the entire person. Emotions and expressive body movements were almost always absent from European religion.

Native healers all through the Americas danced. They allowed the dance to overtake them until the dance began to move the dancer instead of the other way around. The medicine man felt that he had to move with the natural rhythms that sustain life in order to help lead a person from the underlying dysfunction that had led to disease.

I know an interesting story about dancing as medicine!

A white doctor who had moved to Arizona had met a Native American medicine man in the hospital. When he discovered that he and the medicine man were seeing the same patient, the young doctor showed respect and kindness to the old Native healer. He even began to ask the healer some questions about his approach to healing. After a while, the old man began to ask some questions of his own. One of those questions amazed the white doctor.

"Would you show me your dance?"

"What dance do you mean?" the white doctor asked.

"The dance you use to heal people," the Native replied.

"I don't dance," the white man said.

"If you don't dance, then how do you heal?" the Native wanted to know.

In Native thought, movement is life. The spirit is always moving. When movement stops, life also stops. Healing thus involves a restoration of movement, which the medicine man must seek to access.

Perhaps this is a good place to conclude my remarks. The universe is a great system of movement. Things in the universe are moved upon and moved through by the presence of the spirit. When we move as we should, in step with all other things in the universe and in the rhythms given to our particular species, we live our lives in ways that bless and honor the universe. When we move out of step, dishonoring the other parts of the universe, illness and disruptions occur.

I would argue that great disruptions began five hundred years ago in the Americas. One group of people became dislodged from their own soil and in turn dislodged others from theirs. This great disruption has resulted in a continual rape of our planet that has taken us close to the total destruction of all lands and all peoples.

Fortunately, it is not too late to turn back.

The wisdom and forgiveness of the ancient peoples on the American continents can help us return to wholeness with the spirit and thus to harmony with the universe, which is the home of the spirit.

JOURNAL NOTES

I worked for many years with a Hopi pastor. Before I met him, he had been a United States Marine. He had therefore lived a considerable part of his life away from the reservation. However, Hopi was his first language. On 9/11, the local evening news in Phoenix opened with him praying in his native language for the nation he loved.

This loyal patriotic American once told me about how as a little boy he had been playing in the fields when the soldiers came. They arrived in big trucks and gathered the Hopi children while the mothers wailed. It was a terrifying experience because he could not understand what the soldiers were saying.

The trucks took this future marine and pastor to the Phoenix Indian

School. It is now a beautiful place called Steele Indian School Park. Back then it was a boarding school, where the children of the various tribes were forced to cut their hair, wear American clothes, learn the English language, and go to a Christian worship service.

Today, at the Heard Museum in downtown Phoenix, just a few blocks from the old Indian School, one can see pictures of what happened there. After I had visited the museum, I asked my Hopi friend why he was a Christian. He responded with a single word: "Jesus." When he was a child, some Mennonites told him Bible stories and taught him to pray. Something stirred his soul, so he asked for baptism.

He was hardly an embittered man with a grudge. He even thought of himself as politically conservative. He was very devout. Nonetheless, he would shake his head at the ignorance of the crimes perpetrated by the church and the government against his people. His main concern? That the nation's past crimes against his people made it difficult to reach his family and friends with the gospel!

What do American believers do with this part of our history? What do we say about the Western TV shows that demeaned and humiliated the peoples whose land we systematically pillaged? This is a heavy reality that most of us simply choose to dismiss.

Our crimes against Indians didn't bother me either until I pastored in Phoenix. I found out that the sixty thousand Natives who lived in the city were nearly invisible to the evangelical churches that serve the area. When one mentions the Native Americans in conversation, most people just politely change the subject. The great churches that do market research to "reach seekers" rarely even consider the area's original peoples, a group in such need of God and of Christian concern.

Natives die of diseases they first contacted through the diet we forced upon them. They suffer from alcohol poisoning because they cannot find a reason to live sober. If they live on reservations, they remain prisoners of a culture and a language that restricts their standard of living and their opportunities for a better life. If they wander into the cities, they usually live in the poorest of the poor areas, where crime makes their lives a living hell. They are below the last rung on the bottom of our culture's ladder, and they often have no way to even begin the climb.

Telling such people that Jesus died for them and that the people of God love them is difficult. What is amazing is that so many of them do believe. I know that firsthand; I have learned much more from Native believers than they have learned from me.

As with the Jews, it is difficult to critique the religious views of a people whom we have so mistreated. How can we criticize what they have when we have been so unwilling to share our goods, our education, and our churches with them? I realize that these words will strike most Christians as harsh. After all, thousands of Christians love the Native peoples. Unfortunately, most of them are not located near areas where American Indians actually live.

There are, to be sure, notable exceptions. Phoenix alone has two colleges built and maintained by Christians with the expressed purpose of educating Native teachers and pastors. Christians also maintain soup kitchens and used clothing stores. However, very few churches and pastors take an active interest in the spiritual well-being of the Native people. Those that do are woefully underfunded.

I must acknowledge all of this before I offer a critique of Native culture and Native spirituality. But traditional Native religion differs significantly from Christianity, and this requires an explanation.

Believing the Right Thing Is Important

In earlier times, people often debated religion as if their very souls depended on it. As a result, their passion sometimes got out of hand, and people got hurt, abused, or even killed. Opponents of religion delight in pointing this out and are inclined to view all religious passion as irrational and dangerous.

What we miss when we label all religious debate as dangerous—or at least irrelevant—is the fact that all important subjects stir people's passion. When we believe in anything very deeply, it shows. Whether that passion leads us to disrespect others is a matter of maturity and character.

Even in a stable and peaceful democracy, political discussions can easily become heated.

Republicans believe that the nation should be governed more like a republic than like a pure democracy.

Democrats believe the nation should be governed more like a pure democracy than like a republic.

Socialists believe that the infrastructure, goods, and services we own in common are more important than private property and personal rights.

Libertarians believe that we should minimize what we share in common in order to give the individual wide latitude in arranging his or her own life.

Social conservatives are more concerned about what may be lost than about what may be gained from social change.

Social liberals are more concerned about what may be gained than about what may be lost from social change.

If people representing these different perspectives gather at one time in one place, we can hope that their conversation remains congenial and respectful. We will be delighted if each opinion is heard and each person goes away better informed about the other points of view. However, it will not do to tell them that each of their opinions are as good as the others.

Intelligent people know that ideas have consequences and that unlike human beings, ideas are not created equal.

Most people will agree that some ideas are better than others when it comes to politics, economics, or even aesthetics. Most people now do not believe that the same thing holds true for religion. In religion, a civilized man or woman is expected to believe that his or her beliefs are no better that those of other groups. Religion is like cuisine—some people like oysters and some do not, and there is simply nothing to do about that other than to go to the restaurant that caters to one's own taste.

But what if we are wrong? What if religious ideas, no less than political or economic ideas, have serious consequences?

Bishop C. FitzSimons Allison once wrote a beautiful little book called *The Cruelty of Heresy*. It was the first book I had ever read that confronted heresy from a pastoral rather than a theological or apologetic standpoint. Allison began by saying that many heretics have been admirable people, sometimes more likable or even more pious than the ones who opposed them. He admitted that orthodox Christians have often been uncharitable toward those with different beliefs. Nonetheless, he asserted, heresy is cruel because it distorts our view of God, misrepresents God's intentions, and in the long run, undermines the quality of human life.

If Bishop Allison is incorrect about this, then orthodoxy is (as many now claim) merely a manifestation of power. It is in that case an excuse to stifle debate and to squash dissent.

However, if Allison is correct, then a religious leader's lack of passion about theology is not an indication of his or her civility and culture; rather, the indifference shows a profound lack of concern about spiritual health. If heresy harms people as much as the bishop claims, then an unexamined belief system will always breed spiritual disease. Sooner or later, bad theology destroys good people.

That is why people through the centuries have asked such fundamental questions. Does God exist? If He does, is He a person or an impersonal force? Is God a "He," a "She," or something other than either of those things? Do we know what God wants, or is morality whatever we say it is? Has God ever spoken to us? Does He still? Is God even interested in any of us? Does God love us, does He hate us, or is He indifferent?

Religions answer each of these questions (and others like them) in many different ways. The answers we give to the questions create our beliefs, and our beliefs shape how we behave. That makes our answers extremely important.

From a Christian standpoint, Native American religion includes several wrong answers about fundamental questions. The errors affect the way one views nature, the value one places on human life, and the essence of healthy spiritual experience.

Every Native will agree that being a "steward of nature" is very different from being its servant. Being made "a little lower than the angels" or made in the image and likeness of God is very different from being simply one of nature's interdependent parts.[1] Believing one can learn how to transcend time and space to consult with the spirits of nature is not the same thing as cautiously approaching the spiritual world and wrestling against "spiritual hosts of wickedness in the heavenly places."[2]

These differences take people down paths that diverge and finally lead to very different places.

The Native cultures were subdued and supplanted by the European powers. Thus, they did not get an opportunity to develop fully. Unless we count Mexico, the only modern state with unbroken connections to pre-European civilization, no truly independent Native American nation exists today.

When we study Native religion then, we are looking at the shattered remains of a defeated culture. Our views of it thus tend to be re-created symbols that we use for our own needs. Spiritually inclined Americans who for whatever reason are not interested in Judeo-Christian forms of faith may attach themselves to elements of Native culture. So do artistic souls who hope to escape from European convention. Frank Lloyd Wright found inspiration in Native architecture. The men's movement has borrowed Native rites of passage. Some counselors have re-created the vision quest and wilderness journeys. The authenticity of all these Native influences on the culture is suspect and often feels contrived.

Nonetheless, the desire to connect to precolonial American culture can be intense. It can lead people to genuinely convert to viewpoints once considered gone forever. Therefore, Native religion may well enjoy resurgence not only among ethnic Natives but among the descendents of the people who displaced them. For this reason, Christians must take the teachings and practices of Native religion seriously.

In the end, we must ask ourselves what ideas about God, creation, and human worth seem to build healthy civilizations and what ones do not. Given the Native peoples' troubled history, we might seem unfair to say that the ideas and practices proposed by our country's original inhabitants do not lead to a good place. Still, we must be clear. Those ideas and practices may be provocative and even alluring, but in the end, they do not work. And if they do not work, they must be at odds with the way God created the world. We would therefore be cruel to indulge them, whether from a sense of guilt or from nostalgia for simpler times.

Do We Worship the Creation or the Creator?

Native American culture now seems too compelling to criticize. Who will the Christian respect the most, the Native who refused to shoot the buffalo that he did not need, or the European-American who left hundreds of dead bison to decay on the rolling plains? Surely the wise and noble soul who took only what he needed from the earth deserves our admiration. So how can we say that this picture of Native American nobility is unbalanced and incomplete?

We are not inclined these days to recall the dark side of Native life. We find it easy to forget that nature is not always gentle and those who worship her are not always serene. Many a young maiden in ancient Yucatán could testify that Native spirituality was sometimes more respectful of the heavens than of humanity. Many American volcanoes that first provoked awe went on to require blood.

Our modern ecologists, who sometimes urge us to return to the worship of nature, seem unaware of history. The ancient Irish rejoiced when St. Patrick informed them that keeping their fields fertile did not require the lives of virgins. When he told them that one sacrifice had been made for all times, they joyfully untied the last Irish woman who would be sentenced to an early death on the altar. After St. Patrick, the king was no longer expected to sexually mount a mare at his coronation. When fertility became God's concern, the Irish replaced their promiscuity with poetry. For centuries their warriors became scholars who aggressively attacked illiterate Europe with their illuminated manuscripts and their haunting melodies.

As long as the people of Chichicastenango kept sacrificing chickens and lighting incense to the spirits of the dead, poverty and despair settled over their region like a fog. Only when they began to cast aside the demands of nature did nature respond with such bounty that they were finally able to join their nation's newfound prosperity.

A people who worship nature become poor and unlearned. When the sun is a god and the moon is his mistress, the people remain children. From a distance, a culture that revolves around nature may look like Eden, but alas, Eden is as elusive as Scripture claims. Margaret Mead's reflections on the Samoan paradise, where young men and women supposedly came of age unhindered by the restraints of civilization, turned out to be the wishful thinking of an angry Victorian. Naked men in a forest are no more (and no less) noble than suited men in Manhattan.

Nostalgia for more primitive times edits history and creates a myth. One may encounter astounding wisdom in the jungle. I will gladly testify that this is so. However, one also encounters there all the cruelty, vice, and pettiness that abounds on the campus and in the penthouse. A man who worships an alligator is not kinder than the one who worships a bank. Men are men whether "in poverty's vale or abounding in wealth."[3]

Civilization does not create saints, and wealth does not conquer human cruelty. However, when a people learn about law and turn from the capaciousness of shamanism, they do gain a standard against which to judge human conduct. If I learn how to behave from a wolf or a bear, I may become strong and courageous. However, the animals cannot teach me to love my neighbor as myself or to do good to those who despitefully use me. And how will society judge me for killing my rival if the top of the totem is the face of a wolf? Do not wolves kill their rivals? Will they not teach us to do the same?

No wonder one of the Bible's earliest and most emphatic prohibitions is against worshipping nature.

The first chapters of Genesis erupt with the overture: God is not nature, and nature is not God. The prophets repeat the theme in nearly every chapter: Do not bow down to the heavens, do not pass your children through the fire, do not light incense to the oaks. The earth is the Lord's and all it contains. The heavens of heavens cannot contain Him.[4]

The worship of nature, then, is a dead-end street. It leads to nowhere good.

So what is a Christian to believe about the environment? If we do not worship nature, are we free to pillage her? Do we have God's permission to pollute the air and to poison the water? Do righteous people strip the mountains to search for minerals and then leave nature mutilated and spoiled for a million generations? Should we farm animals as we would corn, raising pigs in cells from which they can never escape until the day we turn them into bacon and ham?

Our ecology should not be based on the worship of nature, but that is no reason to rape the earth! The same text that forbids us to worship nature requires us to care for the animals and the plants. We are not free to treat our fields as we like. Every seven years we must allow them to rest. We cannot slay a beast just because we want to kill. Even those we eat must be killed swiftly and humanely. Neither are we allowed to use an animal to satisfy sexual desire. Many commandments like these instruct us about how to treat nature. That is what stewardship is about. We receive resources from our ancestors, and we must cultivate and preserve them for our descendents. At the end of life, God will judge us for our stewardship of the things He has placed in our care.

So Native America offers a path we cannot take. We cannot and must not worship nature. Nonetheless, Native culture rebukes us for not being good stewards of creation. When we observe Native Americans acting from what we judge to be a pagan impulse, and yet they honor the gifts and creatures of God, should we not humble ourselves and admit that we have lost our way on this one important point? Can we really gain the respect of this people, whom we blame for honoring nature to excess, by refusing to honor it at all?

the spiritual smorgasbord:
new age and a new american culture

*The Jews say the Messiah is coming; the Christians say
the Messiah has been here; Einstein said that there is no
time. The truth is, the Messiah is within. It doesn't matter
what we call it or how we frame it. All that matters is that
we claim our inheritance, the power of God to heal and
redeem us. Forget the language. Just build a new world.*

MARIANNE WILLIAMSON

As Walter Summers stepped behind the lectern, I thought he seemed
a bit ill-at-ease. A lady at breakfast had told me that he taught world
history at a high school in Page, Arizona.

Page is the last jumping-off place before one gets to Lake Powell. It is
not a place I would expect to find an intellectual, which I judged Summers
to be.

Maybe that's my problem though. I judge too much, making up my
mind what people are like before I take the time to get to know them. Jesus
told us not to do that—maybe someday I'll start acting like a Christian!

Anyway, Page, Arizona was founded in the late 1950s when workers
needed a place to live while they constructed the Glen Canyon Dam. The
town is on the border of the Navajo Nation, so Native American influence
on the area is quite obvious.

Summers, I learned later, was not a native of Page. He moved there in
the early 1980s from Atascadero, California. He graduated from a small
liberal arts college in San Luis Obispo in his thirties and decided that he
wanted to live in an area with a large Native American population. He had
even learned to speak Navajo—though, as he told me in an e-mail after the
meeting in Phoenix, the Navajos often try to keep from laughing when he
tries to say anything complicated.

He is blond and of medium build, and he wears a pair of round tortoiseshell glasses and one turquoise earring. The morning he spoke, he was carrying a bag made of a rough material—maybe hemp—with a hand-painted sketch of Kokopelli on its side. I kept looking at the bag as he took his notes out of it and prepared to speak.

As I stared at Kokopelli, the enchanting flute-playing deity, I remembered something about him. One Navajo girl had told me in all seriousness that Kokopelli tries to catch young girls alone as they tend sheep. He knows that after he plays his flute, girls lose all their power to resist, and they can end up pregnant.

"This has actually happened to several friends of mine," she said. "All the same, the girls' babies looked like the neighbor boys to me!"

I was smiling at that story when Walter Summers began to speak.

The brochure says that I am presenting the spiritual perspective of the New Age movement. Wouldn't it be great if someone would define what the heck "New Age" is supposed to mean?

Everyone in the room started laughing. We felt a little sorry for him after that remark, and we prepared ourselves to take his talk a little more seriously than we might have otherwise. To tell the truth, when I thought about the New Age movement, all I could come up with was tacky bumper stickers and Jerry Brown!

I'm guessing that the term "New Age" probably evolved from the Age of Aquarius stuff we were singing about years ago under the consider-able influence of mind-altering substances. I guess some of you will remember that the song "Aquarius" was from the musical *Hair*. Most of the cast in that musical got naked onstage. Standing there in a state of nature, they sang "Let the Sunshine In" to the cheers and protests of the American public.

Man, those were heady times! Now we amuse ourselves with these heavy discussions about religion and stuff, which is good, I might add. By mutual but unwritten agreement, most of the people of my generation no longer get naked anywhere except in their own houses, and then for only as briefly and as far away from a mirror as possible. But I digress.

A lady in the back of the room found this remark very amusing and started laughing out loud. I couldn't help but turn to see who she was and noticed that she had turned fire-engine red.

Hey, it happens! Our new prudery is not about morality or religion; it's about the studious avoidance of self-humiliation.

But to continue, the term "New Age" conjures an image of aging hippies in old vans. They are hopelessly naive about life, they eat nothing but tofu and organic carrots, and they ward off misfortune with crystals. I resent this image because I don't have an old van!

The fact is, though, that the spiritual awakening of Western culture is as broad and diverse as any religious movement in history. It emerged as much from serious intellectual influences as it did from the growing desire for spiritual experience among millions of antiestablishment, grassroots baby boomers. Although the movement that spontaneously emerged to meet their need had no real name—except the rather silly term "New Age"—it became the spirituality of choice for a generation of postindustrial, postmodern, and post-Christian Americans.

Contrary to what many people think, the New Age movement is not all fluff. It has a theology and a culture. Like many religions, it claims that it is not a religion at all; it is simply the original way that individuals create a sacred connection to our shared cosmic origins. Since most religions make that claim, I suppose that makes New Age a religion too, albeit a very disorganized one!

That statement may come as a surprise, but hey, if the New Age movement did not have some serious philosophical foundations, it would have disappeared with the hanging beads we used as doors back in the day!

The roots of the New Age movement include the literature of the nineteenth-century Romantics—Wordsworth, for example. I mean, read his "Ode: Intimations of Immortality." A few lines of that poem—my favorite, by the way—will show you what I mean:

> Whither is fled the visionary gleam?
> Where is it now, the glory and the dream?
> Our birth is but a sleep and a forgetting:
> The Soul that rises with us, our life's Star,
> Hath had elsewhere its setting,
> And cometh from afar:
> Not in entire forgetfulness,
> And not in utter nakedness,
> But trailing clouds of glory do we come
> From God, who is our home.

the spiritual smorgasbord

The Romantics were reacting against the growing idea in Western culture of man (and even the universe) as machine. Wordsworth is almost shouting out his defiance: "Trailing clouds of glory do we come / From God, who is our home." Writers like him felt that the church had failed to protect them from the dehumanizing forces of economy and technology that had become Western culture's gilded cage.

The American transcendentalists—Emerson, Thoreau, and the like—were also something like early New Agers. The first hippies—the ones who were really trying to understand the world instead of just smoke dope—devoured Thoreau. He was probably influenced by Native American spirituality. At least his intentional connection to nature makes one think that. Then again, he could have just read Rousseau! Wherever he got his ideas, Thoreau was doing his best to relate to the world very differently from the way most people in Western culture did.

New Age Spirituality Is About Perception

Some of Europe's greatest philosophers laid the groundwork for a new spiritual expression. People like Immanuel Kant and George Wilhelm Friedrich Hegel (don't you wish you had four names?) said things that seriously undermined Europe's older ways of thinking.

John Locke was the last serious philosopher who believed that what we see, smell, hear, taste, and feel is what is actually there. Kant and Hegel announced a new way of thinking, proving that our perception of reality is, at least in part, constructed. That meant that we do not all see the same things or see them in the same ways.

That was pretty heavy!

You can see what that did to Europe's old habit of separating objective from subjective perception. "Subjective" was supposed to mean one's personal opinion. "Objective" was supposedly to refer to what is actually "out there" beyond one's own mind, out in the reality we share with others. A serious thinker would try to be objective. Subjective people, in contrast, were thought of as immature, intellectually unsophisticated, and so forth.

It turns out that we can't be sure about what is really "out there" instead of "in here."

Summers pointed at his head.

This shift in how our culture defines reality was huge. It would inspire Thomas Kuhn to write his famous book about paradigms. That word is terribly overused now, but since New Age folks use it a lot, let me stop to define it.

In the context in which the New Age movement uses it, a paradigm is a network of ideas through which we perceive things. People always work and think within a paradigm. Often, though, they have no idea that their paradigm has been constructed. They just live by their system of thought, assuming that everyone else does the same. But when a paradigm stops working—when it starts to decay—people get really messed up.

An example of this was Archie Bunker. Archie assumed that his mid-century, working-class thought system was simply the way things worked. We laughed at his bigoted remarks and were even fond of him because we recognized something he did not: He was caught in a paradigm that most of his culture had already discarded.

I have to say, though, people say a lot of foolish things about paradigms. If you were to believe some people, you would think that all human perception is constructed. That would mean we could make the world work however we want it to work. (That would be cool, though. I decided once that I wanted my high school students to turn into mushrooms every Friday afternoon. So I closed my eyes and tried to manifest my reality. I haven't got too far with my experiment, but I keep trying!)

No, the material universe actually places considerable constraints on what is possible. Thus, Hopis view reality very differently than Swedes do; both Hopis and Swedes view reality differently than my teenage son does. So most of us now realize that we can view reality in many ways. However, the material world does not bend to accommodate everything our own brains or our different cultures cook up.

Isaac Asimov wrote a story once about a planet where the inhabitants were divided into three genders instead of two. It took three of them to produce a child. (That meant that all three of them had to agree to have sex on the same night. Therapists would become very rich on that planet!) Asimov was a genius. I loved his story. But folks, what he imagined is just not going to happen on our planet, not even to Swedes or Hopis!

So a lot of the popular material about human perception is really nonsense. Nonetheless, that doesn't change the hard-core fact of the matter: The way we perceive things is significantly influenced by our culture, our religion, and our political party. We can no longer pretend that our personal tastes and experiences do not explain much of what we perceive.

So that was the first big thing about New Age thought that I wanted to share: Our inner world determines what we choose to experience in the outer world.

New Age Spirituality Grows from Modern Roots

The next thing to note about the New Age movement is that it is the result of modern scientific discoveries.

Teilhard de Chardin was both a Roman Catholic priest and a pale-ontologist. He became troubled by the apparent clash between his religious calling and his scientific knowledge. The rocks were telling him one thing; his theology was telling him another.

I think that is usually the way our creative leaps begin. We hit a wall because we can't keep pretending that what we wish were true actually is true. Sooner or later, we get tired of the conflict between our different belief systems. Finally, we come to a decision point; either we will commit a kind of intellectual suicide—consciously and deliber-ately ignoring the evidence against our preferred opinions—or we will reject our old belief system. Sometimes, though, we find a third option: incorporating our old way of thinking into a larger frame of reference.

De Chardin chose to accept the evidence of his scientific work. However, he also retained his spiritual sensitivity. As a result, he devel-oped a powerfully compelling system of thought that included the idea of Spirit-directed evolution. In other words, he decided that the universe was indeed a creation. However, de Chardin proposed that a force is pushing creation toward a distant point of completion. This idea was not far removed from Christian teaching. However, de Chardin took his ideas further than what his church could handle. He taught that all things in creation are indwelled by the Spirit, much like the individual believers are indwelled by the Holy Spirit. This permeation of creation by Spirit is total and purposeful, so no element of the universe (nor any era of time) has ever been outside its influence.

De Chardin viewed this process of directed evolution in Christian terms (although orthodox Christians usually do not think so). However, it became quickly apparent that his model did not require that "Spirit" be defined in the same way as the Judeo-Christian traditional beliefs about a personal deity.

The stage was set for growing beyond specific sects and religions to create a more global and inclusive way of thinking about reality. If de Chardin could transcend the differences between science and Christianity, why not transcend the differences between the world religions and cultures in order to share human understanding across cultural and religious boundaries?

This brings me to another important aspect of New Age thinking: We need a spiritual path that does not reject traditional spiritualities but that allows those spiritualities to evolve.

New Age Spirituality Is Evolutionary and Inclusive

As I say this, I am thinking of my neighbor. She is a delightful person and is, I believe, very spiritual. When I was sick a couple of years ago, she asked permission to pray for me. She put some oil on my head and prayed with tenderness and compassion. I was touched by her concern and probably helped by her prayer. So I like this lady a lot.

Not long ago, my neighbor told me that she truly believes that the earth is only six thousand years old! Now, I live beside Lake Powell, a veritable archive of the stages of rock formation. But she was unmoved by my pictures of the strata of fossils imbedded deep beneath the surface of the earth. She seemed unmoved as well by my arguments from DNA studies. With all due respect to this wonderful person, her frame of reference is not much different from what a person would have had during the American Civil War!

Does this make my neighbor a bad person? No! Absolutely not! It doesn't even make her a stupid person. I find her quite intelligent, actually. What it does make her is a woman of Spirit who is trapped in an era that has largely disappeared. She has not, in my opinion, trusted the Spirit to lead her through the scary changes that have taken place since her frame of reference was created. She worries, I think, about her children—really good people—who do not seem to share her views.

My neighbor appears to believe that she is forced to choose between a contemporary world without God and her antiquated world that is filled with Spirit and meaning for her. She has no categories, or so it seems to me, for a spiritually evolved faith that makes room for all we have learned in the past 150 years.

Interestingly, though, my neighbor and her friends use computers. They e-mail one another constantly. I know this because she brings me articles that she prints out, which usually are trying to prove that modern science is wrong. She sees no inconsistency between her use of the products of science and her rejection of the theories and disciplines that make the technology possible.

Taking the principle here a step further, if we need a spirituality that incorporates evolved spiritual perspectives from the past, why should we limit our interest to the spirituality of our own culture or to our recent past? Why shouldn't we explore the spiritual perspectives of other cultures and those of far distant times?

Of course, as we explore other spiritual experiences, we remain the postmodern children of the twenty-first century. It is impossible for us to encounter, say, the Earth Mother, in the same way a person might have encountered her in Central Asia 5000 years BCE!

How then can we experience authentically the spiritual heritage of our planet? In a word, humbly. People like Karl Jung and Joseph Campbell helped us realize that the world's deities do not have to have objective reality for us to value them.

New Age Spirituality Views Deities as Metaphors

This, then, is another feature of New Age experience: the internalization of gods, goddesses, and other spiritual entities as symbols of one's mental domain. This is to be contrasted with the idea that the objective existence of gods, demons, angels, and gnomes must be proved in order for us to value or worship them.

I don't know anyone who has ever seen Thor, not even in Page! However, I met him once in a dream. He came and gave me his hammer. I felt my whole body vibrate with the power of that hammer. I discussed the dream with my therapist; she helped me to fully assume my role as teacher instead of allowing my students to jerk me around.

So does Thor exist? I don't know. Do I have a relationship with Thor? Not really. I do have a painting of him in my den—does that count?

People from more traditional religions visit a New Age bookstore and gift shop and sometimes get freaked out. They see icons of Jesus and Mary. The see copies of the Koran and the Bhagavad Gita. They see crystals, dream catchers, and African masks. They conclude that we don't know what we want or what we believe. They think we are too superficial to commit to one particular path. What they fail to understand is how our openness to all spiritual knowledge—past, present, and around the world—allows us to learn from anyone who has something to teach.

On the other hand, it is true that we are rarely committed to or even interested in the historicity of anyone's sacred stories or in the objective reality of any spiritual being. We say, "Maybe so, maybe not."

Let me tell you what I mean.

New Age Spirituality Is About Experience

I went once to a Native shaman with some friends up in Utah. We drove forever down old mountain roads. Finally we arrived at an old hut beside a very weathered mobile home. When we entered the hut, an old Native man was sitting on a tattered rug. Fortunately, he had plastic chairs for us.

After we had been there long enough for our eyes to adjust to the dark, he lit a pile of sticks in a crude fireplace. They gave off a pleasant odor as they burned. He asked us to watch the fire and then began to speak in some other language—Ute, I think. Then he lit a pipe as he walked around each of us, waving smoke from the pipe as he walked, looking into each of our eyes from time to time.

At some point, he opened a box and removed what looked like a kind of half-baked cake. He tore off several pieces, gave each of us one of them, and motioned for us to eat them. His words grew more rhythmic, and soon I began to see lights of different colors dancing in wonderful patterns around him as he chanted and moved. I don't know how or when, but at some point in the four hours I was with the shaman, I felt the center of my consciousness move to a point above my head. I only know that after that, I watched everything from above the room. I watched as the old man took a swig of Wild Turkey—the whisky, not the animal!—and spit it out on the fire. Then he approached my body—which I was watching from above, you remember—waved his hands over my left ear, and then blew smoke into it.

I had not told him that I was partially deaf in that ear! After that experience in Utah, I have had perfect hearing.

the spiritual smorgasbord

So what did the old man do with all his smoke and whisky? Did he feed us some hallucinogenic? Probably. Did I see what I saw because of neurological intoxication or because the old man knew how to lead me into an altered state of reality? Did I hallucinate, or did I perceive the universe from another point of reference? I don't know. These questions are not important to me.

I have no orthodoxy to protect and no confession to satisfy. I merely experience as much of this brief life as I can. Whatever seems helpful, I use. Whatever seems unhelpful, I avoid. I don't try to explain or judge spirituality; I merely experience it.

New Age Spirituality Is a Culture Change

Naturally, because of the new perspective of our emerging spirituality, we don't live the same way those rooted in a more traditional culture live. We learn that spiritual awareness is dependent upon mind, that mind is dependent upon body, that body is dependent upon organic life, and that organic life is dependent upon the ecological system of the planet—so we tend to become more environmentally concerned. But New Agers are not as worshipful of the earth as people seem to think.

Perhaps you'll be glad to know that I've never actually hugged a tree. My concerns about the environment are really about self-preservation. I want to breathe clean air and drink clean water. I also want my grandchildren to be able to do that. There won't be much of a chance for spiritual growth on our planet if it no longer sustains conscious life!

Believing that masculine and feminine energies have evolved as they have because each contributes something unique to the social order leads us to adopt certain behaviors and attitudes. I mean, think about it: Less evolved forms of life reproduce by dividing themselves in two! That works for them; it doesn't work for us. We have to have voluntary cooperation to conceive children and build families.

Here's a thought. Does an amoeba just get a certain urge one night that it's time to reproduce? Does it sing to itself, "I'm in the mood for love"? Does it have dinner and wine first?

Okay, sorry. Anyway, sexual reproduction requires interaction between a male and a female. Therefore, we may conclude that healthy human society also requires authentic and equal interaction between the genders. So no hierarchy or patriarchy for us. No matriarchy either. We have to learn how to be partners.

Being real partners is not always easy. We are conditioned by the thousands of years we have followed the cultural habits of a patriarchal society. So we need reminders to help us stay on our path in our day-to-day lives. That's why many of us have small shrines in our homes. For example, in a small room just off of our den, Sharron and I have a fountain that we bought in Taos. Over the fountain, hanging on the wall, is a large bronze sculpture of the man in the maze—a popular Native symbol. The sculpture is a symbol for humanity at the core of the cosmos, walking the spiritual journey through life.

In the evenings, the sun comes through our skylight and hits the fountain and sculpture in a way that often moves me to meditate. When I do, I become amazingly centered and aware of myself as a spirit-being. Once I even saw the aura around my hands!

Increasingly, evolved communities are making room for meditation shrines in shared spaces such as hospitals, hotels, and even corporate settings.

Okay, I think that about does it. The New Age movement is a cultural shift in how we experience reality and how we deal with new discoveries, technology, economic advances, fears of ecological collapse—all the stuff of our times. It is not so much a religion as a cultural mood. I suspect that this new spiritual mood influences people in all religions, at least those in the industrial world. The mood is simply a shift of attention away from deities and spiritual forces believed to exist outside ourselves and toward the forces inside ourselves—in our subconscious, or what we used to call our subjective lives.

Whether the New Age movement will actually become a religion of its own or will simply facilitate the synthesis of existing religions and other forces of culture, remains to be seen.

I close with a quote from *A Course in Miracles.*

The holy do not interfere with truth. They are not afraid of it, for it is within the truth that they recognize their holiness, and rejoice at what they see. They look at it directly, without attempting to adjust themselves to it or it to them. And so they see that it was in them...You make the world and then adjust to it and it to you. Nor is there any difference between yourself and it in your perception, which made them both.

A simple question remains, and needs an answer. Do you like what you have made?[1]

the spiritual smorgasbord

JOURNAL NOTES

Many Christian books offer critiques of the New Age movement. For many years the term "New Age" was tossed around within Christian circles to discredit any sort of practice or spiritual discipline that seemed strange to American evangelicals. So a lot of writing and preaching about the movement was available, but much of it was not very informed or helpful. For example, I once heard the term used to discredit prayer practices of Eastern Orthodox communities (even though such practices predate evangelical spiritual practices such as altar calls by hundreds of years.) So the term "New Age" became so elastic to evangelical Christians that it nearly lost any meaning.

If we realize that the New Age movement is simply a modern American version of gnosticism, much of the mystery subsides. In that sense, New Age is anything but new. In fact, it is a most common and basic human spiritual response to nature and life.

When people do not accept the teachings of one of the "revealed religions," their spirituality is likely to lean toward the veneration of nature and the manipulation of consciousness.

The word "gnostic" is related to the English word "know," which is obvious when one writes the two words side by side. As the relationship implies, gnosticism seeks spiritual power through knowledge, particularly knowledge made available by those with "higher forms of consciousness." The gnostic worldview makes the universe a great "chain of being" that stretches from inanimate matter at the bottom to immaterial beings at the top. An enlightened person may steadily gain knowledge from the higher beings and use that knowledge to ascend through (and beyond) nature.

St. Paul dealt with the spiritual ancestors of gnosticism. He denied that Christians could gain spiritual knowledge from angels.[2] He insisted that the spiritual knowledge flows in the other direction: Angels learn about God from Christians![3]

Of course, St. Paul didn't completely eliminate gnosticism from the church. Many Christians remained unconvinced by his arguments, and gnostic strains have influenced Christianity in every century since—including ours.

That brings us to the connection with the New Age movement.

Harold Bloom claims that gnosticism is America's default spirituality.[4] He says that every homegrown religion in our country is based on some sort of gnostic foundation. He claims that Mormonism is a prime example but that many popular Christian movements also borrow extensively from gnosticism.

I think Bloom is right. In fact, our tendency toward gnosticism makes it difficult for many of us to honestly critique the New Age movement. American Christians have the same problem analyzing New Age thought that a fish would have if it tried to analyze water. Our culture—including our church culture—is so permeated with New Age ideas now that Christian orthodoxy itself seems strange to us. Thus the prosperity gospel is deemed Christian while the traditional Eucharist is thought to be pagan.

I heard an advertisement on the radio the other day that illustrates my point. A church in our area—well-respected among Christians for its conservative stance on social issues—was inviting people to visit its Sunday worship services. It promoted itself as a spiritual place to gather, not a religious place.

Wow. Most American Christians will identify with that statement. In fact, the very word "religion" has become offensive to most Americans, believers and nonbelievers alike.

Why?

The word "religion" implies restraint, discipline, communal responsibility, and corporate identity. All of these things sin against the pantheistic and gnostic strains of our national character. Most of us want a spiritual path that meets our spiritual needs as we define them. However, that spiritual path must not restrict our individual expression and must not involve any sense of obligation to others, living or dead. We want an unmediated access to spiritual power and experience. We are often uninterested in scholarly reflections on even our own Scriptures.

So, the mantra "spirituality—not religion" resonates with our national character.

As "religion" has become a hateful word to us, our distrust has grown toward all historical systems of thought and organization. We are not inclined to value Christian art, theology, or liturgy. We are like the generations who came after Joshua, in which "everyone did what was right in his own eyes."[5]

This is the cultural climate in which New Age thought and practice has grown, both inside and outside the Christian churches.

We do well to ask ourselves why this has happened.

In my opinion, it has occurred because Christians in the West came to perceive their scholars and church leaders as arrogant, detached from everyday reality, and unbearably controlling. This is an incomplete and unfair picture, to be sure. However, it is not altogether unfounded. Many Christian thinkers have maligned spiritual experience and belittled piety. Plenty of Christian leaders have been wholly unaccountable, hopelessly out of touch, and terribly disconnected from the spiritual longings of the people they were supposed to serve.

Our theologians have often been guilty of manufacturing obscure jargon, rebuking human emotion, and mocking those preachers who actually made a connection with their listeners. Seminaries have sometimes recruited our best and brightest to perpetrate the disconnect between the pew, the pulpit, and the seminary. This has all worked to make Western Christianity appear to many as an antiquated network of heartless, soulless, and dysfunctional people.

This formidable Christian structure began to appear to its own people as far too complicated and corrupt to reform or to repair. So the people forsook their churches and denominations in favor of warehouses and storefronts.

Once the people experienced celebratory worship (and sometimes a deeper human connection with others) in the newer forms of Christianity, they often rejected their past. The result has been a sort of cultural revolution within evangelicalism. Like China in the late 1950s, American evangelicalism has become intensely anti-intellectual, anti-institutional, and one might even say, anticultural. And, in the United States anyway, many evangelicals have come to define true Christianity as synonymous with social conservatism.

This equation of Christian faith with social conservatism leads many American evangelicals to believe they are theologically conservative when they are merely socially conservative. In other words, if they vote the right way, they must believe the right thing.

The central loyalty of many evangelicals has drifted toward the American civil religion that developed in the years between the Civil War and the assassination of President Kennedy. This civil religion, which connects matters of nation and soul in a seamless unity, is often marked by emotional music and fervent preaching. It is what we once called "the old-time religion," even though this form of Christianity was actually a striking adaptation of Christianity to the American frontier. Nonetheless, it is, in the minds of those who practice it, the "faith which was once for all delivered to the saints."[6]

Cut off from a historical context, evangelicals sometimes misunderstand the nature of their spiritual rivals. The evangelical's reaction to liberal Christianity, for example, is often more about political and social views than about theological ones.

Whatever the reasons, many American evangelicals now tend to be deeply influenced by New Age beliefs. However, because they happen to be socially conservative, they may be unaware of the connection. This is true even of those who preach passionately against the New Age movement.

The evolution of evangelical spirituality into a form of nationalism has made evangelicals enormously successful. Two generations of Americans have embraced evangelicalism in great numbers. But what exactly have they embraced? Have they converted to Christianity or to nationalism? Which of these will win out if and when conflict between the two arise?

The non-reflected nature of evangelical success has also substantially reshaped the organization and practice of evangelical churches.

Evangelicalism's political and social evolution sparked a growing sophistication within the movement in areas such as marketing, structure, and business management. Church leaders became CEOs (or entertainers managed by CEOs), sometimes only slightly interested in spiritual matters. Spirituality became a product to be sold and managed more than a way of life to be embraced. The Charismatic movement, surely a reaction to the loss of spiritual experience in the churches, quickly succumbed to the same reality.

In this context, many spiritually curious people, especially those who were even moderately educated, ceased to view Christianity in any form as a viable option. The mainline churches increasingly felt cold and politicized by the left. The fundamentalists came across as angry with modern life in general and politicized by the right. Seeker-sensitive churches felt like well-oiled machines dedicated to self-preservation and to high-energy entertainment. Charismatic churches looked like carnivals. Christianity in general felt hijacked and marginalized by a global economic machine that had hollowed out the meaning of being human.

Spiritually hungry people had already begun to turn East, toward reinvented forms of native spirituality, toward the post-Christian, secular gnosticism we came to call the New Age movement.

Well, enough of my social commentary! Let's move on to the real issues that separate orthodox Christians from New Agers.

Can Spiritual Symbols Be Mere Metaphors?

I decided while listening to Summers that I had been wrong to dismiss

New Agers as intellectual lightweights. His words contained real content and led to serious implications.

We can easily dismiss people who express themselves with words that have not yet become familiar. Established religions have had centuries to perfect their definitions and concepts. After a while, even those who don't follow those old religions may use their terms. Thus the word "nirvana" is useful to advertisers as well as to Buddhists. The word "redemption" is helpful to ecologists as well as to theologians.

What words are available to secular people if they decide to talk about spiritual things? They often feel that they cannot use traditional religious words because they are so aware of the faults of historical religion. They recall that Pizarro called for Atahualpa's baptism before having the Inca king murdered in Cajamarca. Calvin ordered the execution of Michael Servetus for failing to confess the Trinity. American evangelical leaders called for the assassination of foreign leaders who had opposed American policies. These kinds of stories lodge in the heads of secular souls and discredit the terms they might have otherwise employed.

That is the dilemma of the spiritual awakening we call the New Age movement. Ridiculed by humanists and attacked by Christians, the newly awakened soul of a secular person often employs the language of psychology and sociology. Not yet sure about the objective reality of gods or demons, one can always speak calmly about archetypes and symbols. One can speak to a secular friend about Vishnu or Shiva and know that the friend will understand that he does not refer to the deities as a Hindu might but only as symbols for internal forces within himself. Thus, he can speak of being caught between Vishnu energy and Shiva energy and mean only that he feels conflicted about a desire to create and an opposite desire to destroy.

Karl Jung was the one who developed this modern spiritual language. He created a language that both honors religion and reinterprets it. Jung saw humanity's gods and goddesses, myths, rites and rituals, invocations, and spiritual vocabulary as symbolic ways of describing psychological realities. They were symbols that pointed to forces within what he called "the collective unconsciousness," a substratum of human experience that connected all people in all times and in all cultures.

According to Jung, the collective unconscious was a sea of forces and images created and maintained by the communal memory of human cultures. Just as every nation with a coast has access to all that lives in the world's oceans, so did every individual have access to the collective uncon-sciousness. In dreams, visions, and trance, pictures and symbols might emerge from that primal sea and enter the individual's awareness. Spiri-tuality was about understanding and using this collective information for one's individual needs.

After Jung, even an agnostic could experience and describe spiritual reality without committing himself or herself to a particular faith. In the Jungian scheme, all faiths and all spiritual experiences became the common property of all people. Every man and woman was free to choose and inter-pret the symbols of spirit in the way that seemed helpful to him or her.

This way of looking at spiritual life has become extremely influential in Western cultures. It is, however, a profound problem for orthodox Christians as well as traditional believers of the other monotheistic religions.

For a Christian or a Jew, an invocation of any God but the Creator is forbidden and dangerous. From our point of view, Vishnu, Dionysus, Garuda, Huitzilopochtli, or any being that invites worship and devotion other than the Creator of heaven and earth must be avoided. While secular people may view this attitude as disrespectful, it is actually more respectful than the cavalier and dismissive way that modern people often treat the world's deities. It is even more respectful than the Jungian explanation of the world's religious symbols as metaphors for psychological states.

This difference between the way orthodox Christians and more secular people view religion burst into controversy a few years ago in Vancouver. While visiting the Canadian city, the Anglican archbishop of Singapore, Moses Tay, was shocked to find a totem pole in the courtyard of the Angli-can church. When he mentioned in a sermon that this was a clear violation of the second commandment, a storm of protest spread across the nation. Furthermore, to the great surprise of Anglicans in Canada, the Native popu-lation of the country agreed with the archbishop![7]

The aboriginal Canadians understood that the archbishop viewed their totem as an authentic conduit of spiritual power. It was not, either to them or to him, a cute native trinket or a mere piece of art. It was a sacramental object of a living religion that did not belong in a Christian church.

The controversy sparked a global discussion about the meaning of reli-gion. As the conflict intensified, it became apparent that the secularized Christians of the northern hemisphere had gradually accepted the Jungian definition of religion. Spiritual symbols were expressions of "the language of the unconscious." In other words, for these new kinds of believers, religious ideas and objects were metaphorical ways of describing mysterious psychological processes. Believers in the southern hemisphere, on the other hand, continued to treat religious rites and objects as having inherent power and meaning.

The two viewpoints were poles apart (so to speak) and would not be reconciled. They also formed the foundations of the two opposing sides of a global schism that is now occurring within many of the Christian denominations.

Like revisionist Christianity, the New Age movement accepts the Jungian definition of religion and spirituality. New Agers, however, carry Jungian thought to a logical conclusion. Summers said it clearly in his lecture: If Thor seems to be a helpful symbol of masculine power, then a statue of Thor or an invocation to Thor is a helpful way to access one's psychological energy.

For an orthodox Christian however, to invoke Thor is to invite demonic power into one's life. Just because the Nordic god of thunder has not been worshipped for a while does not mean that some entity will not respond to prayer in his name. Thor may not be a real being, but a demonic presence answers when someone calls his name.

This is what Archbishop Tay meant to communicate in his pastoral address to the churches of Canada. He assumed that the Canadians were ignorant of the biblical prohibitions against the use of alien spiritual objects. He was unaware that they had developed an entirely new language of spirituality that had essentially redefined their Christian faith.

So we see that some forms of Christianity in the northern hemisphere are not far removed from New Age thought. Therefore, revisionist Christians may use words like "Christ," "inspiration," and "grace," but the words often mean different things to them than they meant to their ancestors. The New Age movement merely broadens this process to include anything people find spiritually helpful from any culture. A cry to Aphrodite may enhance sexual experience, and a statue of the Buddha may calm the spirit. So why not use these helpful spiritual symbols?

Orthodox Christians, of course, must face the first commandment. If they do, they will be forced to ask what the injunction could possibly mean if not the literal and apparent sense of the words: "You shall have no other gods before me...for I, the LORD your God, am a jealous God."[8]

So while we should realize that a New Age vocabulary may be the only way some people have to describe their spiritual awakening, we should also not hesitate to warn—with as much tenderness and respect as we can—that spiritual entities are not metaphors and that symbols always embody a power that may not always remain under human control.

Thus, Thor may be powerful; he is not harmless.

What About Evil?

There is a larger question that must be asked of New Agers: Why does the movement seem to have no concept of evil?

A person may understandably get excited about meeting spiritual beings. Ancient spirits that have lived for ages would surely have much to offer us. Why shouldn't we take advantage of them?

The answer is alarmingly simple: Not all spirits are good. Just as every community includes law-abiding citizens, con artists, and criminals, so it is with the spiritual world. Some spiritual beings deceive and corrupt. Furthermore, these spiritual beings are smart—much smarter than we are. If we form relationships with them, we will surely be deceived.

Therefore, the Bible repeatedly warns us against communicating with spiritual beings. God may occasionally send an angel with a special message to a human being. Even then the Scripture warns us to weigh the angel's words against the clear words of Scripture. St. Paul extends the warning to include apostles and prophets: "If we, or an angel from heaven, preach any other gospel to you than what we have preached to you, let him be accursed."[9]

So not all angels are good, and not all spiritual experiences are healthy.

Evil is a force that is far more powerful than human sin. All human beings, even the most holy, are inclined toward sin. We are all born bent. That's why we need a Savior. Evil, however, is an alien virus; humans catch it from intimate contact with fallen angels. As the Lord's Prayer teaches, we can be forgiven of sin, but we must be delivered from evil. Sin is a sickness; evil is an alien life form.

Sin is a weakness of human character. Evil is a strength we may borrow for a season from the world of darkness. The town drunk is sinful and weak; Hitler was evil and strong.

Evil, then, is willful. It seeks to undo things that are good; inflict pain on sentient beings; destroy truth, goodness, and beauty; and humiliate the creatures who bear the image and the likeness of God. In order to do this, evil must somehow convince us to invite its presence into our lives.

Above all, evil seeks to embed itself in cultures and corporations. It seeks to become systematic in order to ease its way undetected into the fiber of human civilization. It worms its way into our ideas so that individuals may work its will without awareness or reflection. It undermines our judgment and manipulates our language. If left unchallenged, it becomes a behemoth that wreaks devastation and opens the doors of death.

When we follow a path that is blind to evil, we become increasingly susceptible to deception. Gradually, we lose our connection to goodness. We begin to erase all boundaries; we obscure all definitions. Good and evil become matters of personal taste and cultural preference. God becomes a metaphor. Life grows exceedingly dark.

Sadly, we must conclude, this is the condition of the New Age movement. It is surely filled with millions of sincere seekers who hunger after God. Nonetheless, it is a global apostasy through which "our ancient foe doth seek to work us woe."[10]

submission to allah:
the way of islam

If you guarantee me six things on your part I shall guarantee you Paradise:
Speak the truth when you talk, keep a promise when you make it, when
you are trusted with something fulfill your trust, avoid sexual immoral-
ity, lower your gaze (in modesty), and restrain your hands from injustice.

AL TIRMIDHI, HADITH 1260

I met Alisher Nurbekov at lunch the day before I heard him speak. I had introduced myself to him because someone told me he was from Uzbekistan. I told him I had visited Tashkent in 1988 and had been intrigued by my first exposure to Central Asian culture.

Alisher seemed shy at first, but he politely answered my questions. He had probably answered them a thousand times for other Americans. "How has the fall of the Soviet Union affected life in Uzbekistan?" "Why did you decide to live in the United States?" "Do you ever visit your homeland?" They are, to be sure, questions that can lead to a deeper understanding of people from other cultures. However, Central Asia remains such a mysterious place for Westerners that even our questions can sometimes come across as though we view its people like some exotic species from another planet.

He told me that he was actually half Tajik and had been raised in the ancient city of Samarqand. His parents had been minor government officials during the Soviet era. He had been educated with Russian and Tajik children in good schools. However, because his family was so connected to the old regime, he had experienced a crisis of national identity when the Soviet State collapsed.

He had always known about the members of his family who had moved to America in the years after the Bolshevik revolution. Then, in the late 1970s, his grandfather was delighted to receive a letter from his brother who

111

had been living in Toledo, Ohio. The correspondence between the elderly men had continued until his grandfather's death in 1985. By this time, several family members were writing to their American cousins. As it turns out, the Nurbekovs had become moderately prosperous business owners. They had a floor covering business at two locations in the Toledo area.

By the early 1990s, Alisher had begun to think about visiting the United States. He mentioned this in a letter to a distant cousin. To his delight, he soon received an invitation to spend the summer in America. More than 20 years before, his great-uncle had created a special fund to help any family member from the Soviet Union who wished to immigrate. This fund enabled him not only to visit America but also to process his immigration should he wish to do so.

After a rapid series of events, Alisher found himself living in Toledo, working at the family carpet business. He enrolled in a certification program for Russian language instructors. He also made friends with some other immigrants at the Islamic Center of Toledo, where Muslims from many different nations had created a community of support and care. Most of them, like Alisher, were from non-Arab nations.

Alisher began his comments with a traditional Islamic phrase.

In the name of God, the compassionate, the merciful.

I am talking to you today about Islam. I am very aware that this is a time of great emotional distance between Westerners and the Muslim world. I don't mind telling you that I am a bit nervous about talking to you.

Mr. McKee asked me to do this presentation after he heard me speak at the YMCA in Columbus, Ohio. A Russian language student from my class in Toledo had asked me if I would talk about Islam at a week of classes that the Columbus Y had organized. I was told that the leaders of the YMCA wanted to inform the public about the Muslim world. One of the organizers, the one who took Russian classes from me, remembered a conversation we had about Islam and suggested that they invite me.

That was the first time I had ever tried to talk about Islam before an audience. I only decided to do it because of my friend. Anyway, for some reason Mr. McKee was there in Columbus and came to the class I taught. After class, he told me about this gathering, and that's why I am here in this famous cowboy place! (I am disappointed that it is modern—not like the old movies!)

Well, I will try to tell you what Muslims believe. Perhaps I can also help you understand why some Muslims have become angry with the West. I ask for your understanding as I do this. It is a very delicate subject, and I wish to explain myself without bringing you any distress or offense.

I also will welcome any questions you may have when I conclude my remarks.

I am a Muslim now, but I was not raised in a religious family. My parents were actually members of the Communist party. They viewed the Muslim roots of our people as a "superstitious stage of human development," as my uncle once put it.

My first real exposure to Islam came through a Russian atheist schoolmate. I had been talking with him about the Persian empire and the Islamic state that came after it. (You know, in Samarqand, one cannot escape the many reminders of the great Persian and Greek empires! I hope all of you will go sometime to our great city and see it for yourself!)

Anyway, this Russian friend remarked that he had seen a copy of a book in the school library that might interest a Farsi-speaking person like me. It was a summary of Imam al-Ghazali's *Revival of Religious Sciences.* He said that this man had been some great intellectual in the Abbasid era. So the next day, I went to the library and found the book. It was in Russian—unfortunately, a very stilted and old Russian at that—but I decided to read it anyway. I didn't actually understand much of it, you understand, but reading it felt so subversive! Here I was reading something that my Farsi-speaking ancestors would have thought valuable but that was so foreign to my young Russified, Socialist culture! I plowed through the book, writing down any phrases and concepts that I could not understand.

I was hoping, I think, to discover something to use to annoy my parents at dinner time!

A few weeks after I had started reading al-Ghazali, a fellow student invited me to visit her family's home in Bukhara during winter break. While I was there, her brother took me to the burial place of Bahauddin Nagshbandi (may God sanctify his secret). He was a Muslim saint who lived in the fourteenth century. For decades, the government had used his mausoleum as a warehouse, but religious people visited it anyway.

I saw an inscription on the wall that I could not read. It was in

Farsi, but of course it was written in the old Arabic script. (The Soviet regime replaced our old script with the Cyrillic alphabet so people educated after the revolution were unable to read the thoughts of their ancestors.) I kept staring at the words until an old man came by to see what I was staring at. He smiled at me. He then whispered the words, *"Dil ba er, dast bakor."* It means, "Heart in love; arms in labor." I repeated the phrase after he had spoken it. Then he just kept on walking.

Afterward, the phrase would spontaneously erupt inside my head. *Dil ba er, dast bakor.* As I would discover later, the phrase meant that holiness involves practical life, not just mystical experience. In other words, healthy transcendence provokes practical transformation. That idea captured my thoughts. I still meditate on it often. I had always assumed that mystics were simply unbalanced. Now I had seen that one of our greatest mystics actually warned against any mysticism that does not result in a wholesome practical life.

In this new frame of mind, while still in Bukhara, I bought a poorly printed copy of *The Conference of the Birds* by Farid al-Din Attar. As I read it, I became steadily convinced of a reality beyond our material world. I also realized that I needed instruction about how to deal with this new discovery. That's why when I returned to Samarqand, I went to a mosque. I told the first person I met there that I wanted to speak to a teacher. Although I had not yet realized it, I was about to become a Muslim.

So what is Islam? That is what you want to know—so enough of my personal story!

Although in one way of speaking Islam is as old as the world—for "Islam" means submission to God—the global movement we specifically call Islam was born in the year that the Western calendar refers to as AD 610.

Muhammad (God's blessings and greeting of peace be upon him) was a well-respected trader from the sacred city of Mecca. He was in a cave on Mt. Hira, meditating on the economic injustices of his society. Although he had profited by the commercial structure of his clan, he had never forgotten that he had been an orphan. He had tasted life from the margins of the world. Although he had married well and had highly respected relatives, he had come from difficult beginnings. He had to figure out what all this meant for him.

As he meditated, suddenly he was overcome by awe. Then he heard a voice commanding him to read.

"But what shall I read?" he asked of the voice. The prophet was especially fearful because he could not read.

Then the voice spoke again. "Say in the name of the Lord Creator, who created man from a single cell. Say that the Lord is most Beneficent. He has taught the use of the pen. He has taught man what he did not know."[1]

The prophet was hearing the voice of Gabriel, the same angel Jews and Christians revere as God's messenger.

Muhammad (God's blessings and greeting of peace be upon him) was, like many of God's messengers, a most reluctant prophet. He struggled furiously against the idea of becoming a spiritual messenger. In the prophet's day, you see—as in ours—mystically inclined people were not always respected.

In the culture of ancient Arabia there were individuals called the "kahin." These people were essentially seers, people who entered shamanistic trance in order to access divine knowledge for their clients. These kahin often gave their messages in mysterious and cryptic verses. Although most Arabs used them, they also disdained them. This was especially true of Mecca's most powerful clan, the Quraysh, of which Muhammad (God's blessings and greeting of peace be upon him) was a member.

As the months went by however, the Qur'an—or recitations, for that is what the word "Qur'an" means—continued to come.

I am sorry that I don't have time to tell you all the history of the prophet's life. On the other hand, it is the spiritual story, the steps the messenger took to become God's servant, that is my focus today. For although none of us can become Muhammad (God's blessings and greeting of peace be upon him) because he was, after all, the seal of the prophets, any human being can become a servant of God. Indeed, we are all called to so that. We are all called to Islam—to submission to God.

I do have time to tell you that at first his home city of Mecca rejected the prophet. Its powerful ruling clan, the Quraysh, were threatened by the egalitarian society that the recitations from God prescribed. Their opposition to his ideas turned violent, so he decided to leave the city. When Muhammad (God's blessings and greeting of peace be upon him) and all his followers were offered refuge from the peoples of Yathrib, the prophet led his followers out to a new home, just as Moses had led his people long before. We call this exodus from Mecca the "Hijra." Its occurrence marks the first year of the Islamic calendar.

It was in Yathrib, soon to be known as Medina, that Muslims (or people submitted to God) became a real community. We call this community the "umma." The umma at Yathrib would serve as a model for Muslim culture through the centuries. So this period is an important focus for Muslim studies. However, in time, the rulers of Mecca were not content to leave the new umma in Yathrib alone. Its very existence was a threat to them. So they sent armed men to subdue the Muslim community by force. Of course, these raids were unsuccessful. Ultimately, Muhammad (God's blessings and greetings of peace be upon him) walked back into Mecca with thousands of his followers. This time, though, he entered as its ruler.

Once in Mecca, the prophet destroyed the idols of the "Ka'ba"— the ancient place of Arabic pilgrimage. He put an end to the old way of life—the pre-Islamic culture that Muslims call "Jahiliyyah." In its place arose a new society dedicated to justice and righteousness.

In the time the prophet had left on this earth, the various tribes of Arabia began to submit to the governance of God and to his prophet. To do so, they had only to recite what we now call the "Shahada:" "I bear witness that there is no god but God; I bear witness that Muhammad is God's messenger."

This simple invocation became the way of entrance into the Islamic community. It is the same declaration I recited before several witnesses in Samarqand just a few weeks after my trip to the tomb of Naqshbandi (may God sanctify his secret).

The Shahada thus becomes a new beginning for a person, much the same way as the Ka'ba became new after the prophet cleansed it of its idols. For in a real sense, every person is born a Muslim, born submitted to God. Our perverted cultures fill men and women's hearts with idols. In order to submit to God, people must cleanse themselves from those idols. The Shahada is where we begin this work; it is how we acknowledge our submission to the ways of God.

By the way, I have been using the English word "God" because that is the language we are speaking here. However, as most of you know, Muslims usually use the Arabic name for God—"Allah." We do that because that is the name used in the Qur'an. However, we do not worship another God other than the one true God whom Jews and Christians also worship. In fact, the word "Allah" is linguistically connected to the Hebrew word for God. Arabic-speaking Jews and Christians use this same word for God—"Allah"!

After confessing the Shahada, converts learn to express their submission to God through the "Salat," or daily prayer. Whenever possible, Muslims pray in community, in the way prescribed. This creates a certain rhythm and symmetry among worshippers. A Muslim can thus go anywhere in the world where there are other Muslims and worship with them with total ease and familiarity.

The building where Muslims maintain their community life is often called in English a "mosque," from the Arabic "masjid." Actually, Muslims do not require a building at all for their spiritual life. Nonetheless, the mosque is very important to us.

The internal arrangement of a mosque is much like that of a synagogue or a Christian church. In the place of the Torah or the tabernacle, however, is a simple niche to indicate the direction of Mecca. To the right is a podium, as in the older Christian churches and synagogues. Like Jews and Christians, we use our pulpits for giving sermons.

Muslims are required to help the poor. So we give a special offering called the "Zakat," or alms. Because it is as important to us as prayer, it is obligatory.

We also keep a fast during the month of Ramadan. During this fast, the "Sawm," we do not eat, drink, or have sexual relationships until after sundown.

Finally, Muslims are called to make a pilgrimage, or "Hajj," to the city of Mecca and to pray at the Ka'ba.

These five things—the Shahada, Salat, Zakat, Sawm, and the Hajj—constitute what are often called the five pillars. The attitude with which we carry them out is called exertion, or "jihad."

I noticed how the room suddenly grew tense as Alisher said the word "jihad." He noticed it too. After a few seconds, he continued.

I realize that this word has unfortunate connotations for most of you. I am deeply sorry about that. For the vast majority of Muslims, "jihad" refers to the intense struggle one must undertake to be God's servant. It can also refer to the forceful movement of our faith into new cultures.

But this is of course a commitment that Muslims, like Christians, believe to be a part of their spiritual responsibility. In no context should "jihad" refer to murder and mayhem. Those kinds of things create a very different kind of people than what we must strive to become. Jihad should first be a struggle with our own being, exerting our strength to submit to God.

Now I must say to you—and this is extremely important—that one could do all the important things I have mentioned without ever really becoming submitted to God. A servant of God must be more like someone smitten with love, you see, than like someone forcibly subdued.

So how do we become submitted to God? Well, we must understand that God is one—He is "tawhid"—and has no parts and distinctions. (In this we differ from Christians, who envision God as having parts.) However, if God's nature is characterized by oneness, or tawhid, then those who worship Him must also become steadily aware of their essential oneness with Him and with one another. If God is one, what could possibly exist that would be other than God?

(Not all Muslims would be comfortable with my putting it quite this way. But it is the way I first learned to envision my love for God back in my own country, so I offer it to you.)

I am trying to say that our journey toward God involves not only our outward observances but also an inner journey. We call this spiritual journey "tariqah." It is what captured my imagination when I first read *The Conference of the Birds*.

The famous Persian parable tells us that our walk toward God takes us through a number of stages. Each stage helps unmask the illusions that have kept us separated from God. First we hunger for righteousness, as Jesus Himself said. Then we experience love. We turn another corner of our life and encounter mystery. We move on to detachment, where all our certainties get shattered. We slowly discover unity and then leave behind the emptiness of our old definitions and boundaries—things that divide us from one another and from God. Finally, we come to a state of "fana," or ecstasy, where we leave behind our sense of self and truly experience tawhid—divine oneness.

The great classic *The Rubaiyat of Omar Khayyam* describes this state of tawhid as ecstatic love. It is the state many human beings strive to reach through drugs and immoral lives and in many other kinds of idolatrous ways. In the end, though, none of these things satisfy the soul. They obscure, rather than reveal, God's oneness—tawhid.

When I first began to yearn for this sort of relationship with the divine, my teacher in Samarqand taught me to repeat the sacred names of God in prayer. So I joined a group of seekers who had been taught to repeat the sacred names until the words themselves disappeared and only ecstatic speech remained. When this happened to me, I knew what all my reading and study actually meant. Until that time, my ideas and thoughts had been mere signposts. They pointed to the reality of that eternal word that is the source of all human reflections of God's word, but they were not the reality itself. With my friends in Samarqand, I discovered more than religious teachings about God—I discovered God Himself!

The Qur'an

Of course, I must say something about the Qur'an. Muslim respect for the Qur'an is often compared to the Christian's view of the Bible. But I think that our connection to the Qur'an is something quite different. To the Christian, a Bible is the word of God pouring through the people of a certain time and culture. Thus, the Bible is written in the words and style of the author's culture and era of history. A Muslim, however, thinks of the Qur'an as more like Christians think of Jesus—the Word of God made flesh. The Qur'an is unmediated; it did not flow *through* Muhammad; it was delivered *to* Him. It was not in any way constructed by him, in other words. The angel's phrases and cadence were as purposeful and eternal as the thoughts they expressed.

For this reason, the Qur'an cannot really be translated; it can only be interpreted. There are good English interpretations of the Qur'an, and they can be useful to a seeker of God. However, they are not the Qur'an. At best they are like defective mirrors that reflect something of the grandeur and glory of the original.

With that, my time has come to an end, and so I look forward to meeting with anyone who would like to discuss more about Islam.

JOURNAL NOTES

First, I want to address my social and political issues with Islam. I tried to listen to Alisher with an open mind, but that was hard to do. I couldn't seem to forget where I was and what I was doing on September 11, 2001. That was unfair to Alisher, but what can I do about it?

I have been reading Karen Armstrong's *The Battle for God* (2000, Knopf). The book is something of a sequel for her previous work, *A History of God,* in which Armstrong compared the theology, mysticism, ritual, and philosophical worldview of Jews, Christians, and Muslims. In the later book, she describes how fundamentalism has arisen in each of these religions as reactions to global secularism. These groups sprang into being, she says, because some Muslims, Christians, and Jews have a visceral fear that modern societies are destroying the religious perspective through which they view the world and live their lives.

Reading Armstrong's book, I was amazed to discover that many devout Muslims have been feeling what I often feel—that the modern world has left no place for the attitudes, worldview, and social structures in which I was raised and from which I derive my sense of place in the world. And yet I am a modern man. I can't really be anything else. So the conflict is not only between my view of the world and those held by others. The greatest conflict is between the conflicting worldviews within my own self. That is the dilemma faced by all traditional religious people educated and living in a world that has been shaken by the secular earthquakes.

This means that I can relate to a conservative Jew or Muslim's sense of "deracine" (a French word meaning "uprooted"). That word expresses for me the sense of violence and vulnerability that religious people often feel in the new world order. When something severs a plant's root system, that plant is going to be in real trouble. That is the sense of vulnerability that many religious people feel around the world.

As Armstrong points out, most modern individuals experience secularization as a freedom from prejudice, fear, legalism, and superstition. However, religious people often experience secularization as a spiritual vertigo; the world seems to spin around until one is left reeling.

Technological advances help us live longer, and they extend human life further into the universe. But if a longer life and a limitless universe have no meaning, religious people may be forgiven for asking why a longer life and a longer reach were so important in the first place.

That question of meaning, so fundamental to spiritual people in ages past, seems to rarely surface in our times. Believers sense that as the secular world's tolerance for religion shrinks, they should downplay their faith. Especially when making decisions about culture and career, they must remain quiet about the source of their beliefs. Many traditional religious believers even feel they have been uninvited to the global culture. Nonetheless, the questions about meaning and purpose persist.

Muslims have an added burden of experiencing secularism as a foreign invasion. This means that "progressive" (secular) Muslims must not only keep their faith private, they must adopt the clothing of foreign peoples to prove that their loyalty is to the emerging world culture and not to the past religious roots of the region. I don't think I ever really thought about that before reading Armstrong's book. She encourages secularization, but she understands the heart of a traditional believer and helped me see that this is not just a conservative Christian's dilemma.

Could this widespread concern about secularism teach me to empathize with people who feel the same concern? After reading Armstrong, I felt some sense of understanding for Muslims that I had never felt before. In many ways, their anxiety about finding a place in the emerging world is not so different from what I feel at times. Perhaps knowing that we share some of the same concerns could make the world a safer place.

Theological Issues with Islam

Most Christians seem unaware of the roots we share with Islam.

Like us, Muslims believe that the universe was created by one supreme being. This belief implies a view of the world in which math and science are possible. For if all things were created by one supreme being, we should be able to discern design and structure in the universe. That belief is implied by the very word "*uni*verse," which conveys the notion that all things, regardless of how different they are from one another, are nonetheless traceable to a single cause. Muslims, sharing this belief with Jews and Christians, made valuable contributions to Western culture's emerging sciences.

Furthermore, like Jews and Christians, Muslims believe that the things God created can submit to God but cannot become God. Therefore, we are philosophically in agreement with Islam at more fundamental levels than we are with pantheists, animists, and followers of other non-monotheistic religions.

Once we get over our fear of Islam, we see that the ways Muslims view the world and live their lives are often very close to what we would expect of an Old Testament people. In fact, there is much about Islam that should remind us of St. Paul before his conversion. But this philosophical connection also points to our most basic difference with Islam. Obviously we do not regard Muhammad as God's messenger and we do not receive the Koran (I will use the anglicized spelling) as God's word. However, we see an even more basic reason why we must reject Islam as a valid pathway to God: It teaches that human beings can win their way to God through their own righteousness.

Submission Is Not the First Principle of Spiritual Life

The core idea of Islam is submission to God. Indeed, that is what the word "Islam" means. Some Christians may be shocked that I do not believe that submission is the essence of Christian or Jewish spirituality. We must submit to God, of course; we must acknowledge His sovereignty and lordship over our lives. However, the most basic belief of the New Testament is not submission but rather love and relationship.

In the Old Testament book of Job, we are startled to find Job, page after page, arguing with God. In contrast, Job's pious friends submit—even grovel. However, when God finally speaks at the end of the book, He commends Job. He calls Job His friend! Only Job, God says, had spoken the truth about how he felt toward God. The others did not really know Him, despite their passionate words about proper theology and obedience.

This leads us to believe that God is after real relationship with us rather than our servile flattery and sentimentality.

Young children must submit to their fathers. However, as they mature, even good children will argue with their fathers. Indeed, good fathers will encourage the argument as long as the children speak with respect and keep the argument within proper boundaries. This is because a healthy father does not seek his child's mindless submission; rather, he wants the child to grow into a mature human being. Masters of slaves ask for submission; fathers ask for growth and authentic relationship.

Muslims find this train of thought troubling. Unfortunately, so do many Christians. Too many Christian leaders define piety as submission to God's representatives. Pastors, denominations, doctrine, and church policies can all claim sovereignty over us and threaten us with damnation if we fail to submit to them.

Of course, any group has a right to define itself. For example, a denomination has a right to say that a member of the group must not drive red cars or wear brown hats. If people want to belong to that group, they must abide by those rules. However, a group that requires people to keep these rules in order to remain in Christian fellowship becomes at best peripheral to the Christian faith and comes precariously close to excluding itself as a legitimate expression of Christianity. It becomes more like a sect and perhaps even a cult.

Christian life, then, is about walking toward spiritual maturity. We wrestle with Scripture and learn to apply the Word of God to the affairs of life. We do this when we vote, when we make business decisions, when we marry, and even when we prepare for our death. To mature, however, we need freedom to think, speak, and act. We need freedom to experiment with our beliefs, even if our experimentation results in failure or embarrassment, spiritually speaking. The worst thing is not to make a mistake but to fail to grow.

When we teach compliance and submission as our first spiritual principle, we misrepresent the nature of God. God's ego is not served by human compliance. God's desire is for us to become His eternal companions. For that to happen, we need relationship with Him.

Human beings who claim to speak for God but then require submission to their system simply do not speak for the Almighty. They speak out of their own personal anxiety and out of a need to control others. "Beware the people who are always standing on the truth," Paul Garlington once said. "Sooner or later, they will want to stand on you!" Legalism leads to tyranny—not sometimes, but every time.

A healthy submission to God thus is the result of an informed struggle with truth and relationship. It is a response to love, not a capitulation to power. In contrast, people who make submission the first principle of spiritual life will seek to create compliant populations who are expected to remain content even under the most terrible despotism and abuse.

Islam, like many misguided forms of Judaism and Christianity, is a form of legalism, a way of trying to find favor with God by doing the right things. Therefore, all the arguments that the New Testament makes against rabbinical Judaism are relevant when speaking about Islam. In fact, in one passage, St. Paul speaks about the bondage of Hagar and her children in Arabia. In this passage, Paul is referring metaphorically to rabbinical Judaism of course, but his image is more than apt where Islam is concerned.

"Stand fast therefore in the liberty by which Christ has made us free, and do not be entangled again with a yoke of bondage," St. Paul writes.[2]

The law is good and upright. However, human beings are fundamentally flawed. Without a relationship with God, we simply cannot carry out the law. Therefore, we have it backward when we make submission the first step of a relationship with God. If we were naturally able to submit to God, we would have submitted a long time ago.

New Testament Christianity teaches that the first order of spiritual business is not submission that leads to relationship but rather a relationship that enables submission.

Consider this passage: "God demonstrates His own love toward us, in that while we were still sinners, Christ died for us."[3]

The Koran denounces the ungodly because it views sin as a deliberate affront to God. The New Testament, seeing sin as the involuntary fruit of a twisted human nature, offers compassion and healing for all who sin. Therefore, Jesus begins His great Sermon on the Mount by saying, "Blessed are the poor in spirit." That is, blessed are those who realize that they lack the ability to respond to God.

We, the addicted, the shamed, and the sinful are all welcomed by the Carpenter who was Immanuel, "God with us."

Muhammad claimed that Allah did not want sinners unless they straightened up first. However, Jesus said, "Come to Me, all you who labor and are heavy laden, and I will give you rest."[4] One path tells us to get good so we can meet God; the other path invites us to meet God so we can become good.

Christians Cannot Accept Muhammad as God's Prophet

A Christian can and should respect Muhammad. Although we cannot receive Muhammad as God's messenger, we can respect him for having extended God's moral code into Arabic culture. As a result, systems of jurisprudence developed within that vast portion of the world. Muslims are people of law; they revere a written source of law derived from Moses. This allows them to appeal to justice and equality. Law comes from God, so people are blessed when they accept the law. Muhammad taught people to respect God's law, and as a result, his world became a better place. He is certainly worthy of respect for doing that.

Muhammad also founded a culture. He left the Arabic world a much different place than he found it. He ennobled the Arabic language and gave it its first real literature. To Arabic-speaking people, the Koran is the King James Version of the Bible and the works of Shakespeare, Milton, and Spencer all together. So we can also respect Muhammad as a founder of a civilization.

We cannot honor Muhammad as a prophet, however, because the canon of Holy Scripture closed with the writing of the New Testament. The same Spirit who inspired the apostles to write the New Testament also inspired the church fathers to recognize, select, and seal God's written revelation to humanity. Since then, writings and prophetic utterances may be inspired in a certain sense; believers may love them and use them extensively. They cannot however, be regarded as Scripture. Thus, books like *The Imitation of Christ,* one of the most beloved pieces of literature in Christian history other than the Bible, nonetheless remain outside the Bible. They are not Holy Scripture. Even the Apocrypha, an extremely important collection of Jewish writings that many believers read on a regular basis, is not Holy Scripture. Although Roman Catholics and Orthodox Christians print the books of the Apocrypha in their Bibles and use them for public readings, even they must not give the Apocrypha the same level of respect as the Old and New Testaments receive.

We therefore reject Muhammad as a prophet for the same reason that we must reject Joseph Smith and Mormonism, Mary Baker Eddy and the Christian Science movement, and Brother Billy Bob's revelation that we should all dress in white and wait on a mountain for the coming of the Lord. The canon of Scripture is closed. No person, whether Jew, Christian, Muslim, or Martian, can add a single word to its witness.

All prophets and seers who speak in the name of the Lord must speak only that which agrees with the common witness we have received from the apostles. All orthodox Christians agree with this statement, from Catholics to Copts, from Baptists to Mennonites, from Pentecostals to Presbyterians. Neither the Book of Mormon, the Koran, *A Course in Miracles,* or, for that matter, Scofield's notes on the Bible are anything more than human opinion, which must be weighed and discerned in the light of Holy Scripture. (Scofield certainly would have agreed!)

We must also reject Muhammad as a prophet because of his inaccurate depiction of Jesus Christ. We realize that Muslims honor Christ as a great prophet, and we are grateful. We can find common ground with some Muslim groups, particularly the Sufis, who encourage people to follow the teachings of Jesus. Nonetheless, the New Testament presents Jesus not only as a prophet but as the Savior. Christ is not only a great man; He is the incarnate God.

Jesus, as we confess in the Apostles' Creed, "suffered under Pontius Pilate, was crucified, died, and was buried...The third day He rose again from the dead." Muslims deny this. In so doing, they fail to grasp the wonder of grace and the freedom of relating to God through His uncon-ditional forgiveness.

In short, Muslims have no mediator between God and man and thus no supernatural power to transform the human soul. A book, even a wonderful book, may show us how to live, but it cannot change us. We are not changed by forcing ourselves into new behavior; we are led into new behavior by the sort of profound change we call transformation. This profound change, through which we are made into new creatures, requires a radical renewal of human nature. This is made possible only through the death of the God-man, who now represents us before the high throne of heaven.

Islam Seeks to Become a State

We must also reject Islam because it is a religion that seeks to become a state. Although Christians have often violated the Bible's teaching on this, the New Testament clearly teaches that God grants the state a different authority than He gives the church. Thus, the church must not seek to be a state, and the state must not seek to be a church.

Although some American Christians now speak angrily about the sepa-ration of powers, the doctrine was not a principle of humanism. It was a product of Protestant Christianity. The doctrine is vital to our faith because it protects human freedom and makes clerics as well as governors account-able to human law.

In the mysterious and cryptic conclusion of the Bible, we find a word picture of a prostitute who rides a beast. The writer expects us to compare that woman with another woman in the same book. The other picture is of a bride, adorned with glory and grace. The bride obviously signifies the community of Christ, so we are left wondering about the whore's identity. When we realize, however, that the beast is meant to represent human government, we see that the prostitute is simply a woman who could have been—and should have been—a bride. However, she prostituted herself by riding the back of the beast. She sought power instead of purity and thus disqualified herself from becoming who she was meant to be.

The book of Revelation thus leaves us with a warning about what hap-pens to a spiritual community that falls in love with temporal power.

Believers must be just, and they must work for justice on the earth. They must be moral and encourage the moral health of their communities. How-ever, believers cannot force unbelievers to live by their code of life. When they try to do this, they engage in a kind of spiritual prostitution. They set up a system in which believers must try to force unbelievers into compliance with the values of the kingdom of God. However, a coerced righteousness is not righteousness at all. Its results are spiritually useless.

This, then, is another fundamental separation between the ideals of Islam and those of Christianity. Priests are not meant to be presidents, and governors are not meant to be gurus. Believers live by their faith in the private and the public realms of their lives. However, believers must not use public offices entrusted to them to bully or control others in the name of their religion.

Through the eyes of a Christian, Islam is an attempt to gain God's favor through legalism and through submission to a state that acts in the name of the Koran and Islamic tradition. As in all forms of legalism, this submission must be enforced through surveillance, manipulation, and coercion. In such an atmosphere, men and women are not likely to become free moral agents who can choose God because of their conclusions drawn by their informed conscience.

As in all forms of legalism, Islam often provokes primal rage, promotes profound hypocrisy, and produces irreconcilable differences over insignificant things. Furthermore, it seeks the power of the state to enforce its legalistic views. As we stated earlier, all this can be said of Christian and Jewish legalism as well, as indeed the books of Romans and Galatians clearly say.

Islam describes God as absolute oneness without internal distinction. This view impacts Islamic culture in ways that discourage freedom. If God does not take counsel within His own being and does not accept input from His subjects, we are left with no model for legitimate diversity and dissension among human beings. The Islamic view of God thus leads one to define unity in society as uniformity. Serving one God without internal distinctions leads a people to expect that a healthy culture will not tolerate internal distinctions. The "unim" devours the "pluribus."

We must admit that Christian life seldom lives up to Christian teaching. Still, because we believe that the one God is at the same time Father, Son, and Holy Spirit, we are prepared to consider that one Church may be at the same time Anglican, Baptist, and Pentecostal. Our lack of institutional unity is not supposed to lead us to conclude that those outside our group are not real Christians, although in practice it often does.

Conclusion

In the end, Islam includes much that a Christian may sincerely affirm:

submission to allah

jihad defined as a war against our own fallen human nature, God's one-ness, God's sovereignty, and the importance of human law as a gift from the Almighty. We can also honor Islamic contributions to civilization: the revival of classical learning after centuries of European illiteracy and super-stition, algebra, astronomy, and our number system, particularly the zero! Finally, we can learn from those centuries when Islamic cultures treated Jews and Christians in ways that were much more mature and godly than the way Christian cultures treated Muslims and Jews.

As people made in God's image and likeness, Muslims certainly deserve our respect. They too are children of Abraham and, like Jews, are our spiri-tual kin. However, we cannot view them as members of the household of faith. We can confess with them that "there is no god but God," but we cannot complete their sentence to say, "and Mohammed is his prophet."

Rather, we must say, "There is no other god but God, and Jesus is His only begotten Son, through whom alone we may have eternal life."

sole judge of truth:
the path of secular humanism

Know then thyself, presume not God to scan
The proper study of mankind is man.

Created half to rise and half to fall;
Great lord of all things, yet a prey to all,
Sole judge of truth, in endless error hurl'd;
The glory, jest and riddle of the world.

ALEXANDER POPE

*R*ussell Thomas Burtrano...*sounds like someone who went to an Ivy League school and takes vacations in Europe,* I thought as I read the brochure.

Burtrano was not giving a formal presentation at this conference. He was a presenter at one of the few optional evening sessions. Few of the symposium participants seemed to be interested in these optional discussions. We were generally too exhausted by our morning and afternoon sessions to return for more lecture and discussion. However, I had decided to attend Burtrano's discussion group.

I admired the self-declared humanist, whose views on religion would probably offend all of us, for his willingness to attend our sessions and listen respectfully to the speakers. His questions and comments in the sessions had been frank but kind. He had avoided the sarcasm toward religions that I had come to associate with people of his intellectual disposition. That's why I decided to go hear him.

> First, let me thank you for coming this evening. I know that you are tired. You must be here because you sincerely want to hear the opinion of a person whose ideas challenge the beliefs you hold dear. That is respectful and courageous. So I thank you.

129

I suppose the best place to begin is by acknowledging the positive role religion plays in the world.

First, religion provides a comprehensive view of the world. It allows people to connect the parts of their lives and create a common culture. Although I tend to disagree with many of Samuel Huntington's conclusions in his unfortunately influential book *The Clash of Civilizations,* I agree with his assertion that the world's cultures have evolved out of religious perspectives.

Culture has to begin somewhere. If we are to live together at all, we must have a theoretical framework that encourages the emergence of economic, governmental, and educational systems. From these things a culture evolves its systems. Religion is thus usually, and probably always, the first step in the process of constructing a culture. Only a religion had the power to make legitimate the social structures that united and organized ancient people.

The question I must press upon you, however, is about the *permanence* of religion. My first academic degree (the one that led to my first job) was in social work. The reason I studied sociology was because I had a girlfriend in the eleventh grade who had decided to pursue sociology. Frankly, I wanted to impress her; so I started talking about social work and showing an interest in the causes that interested her. We dated for a couple of years while I was choosing my first college courses. After we split up, I was already genuinely interested in social work. This means that my professional interests were greatly influenced by a young lady whom I still remember fondly but who did not turn out to be my life companion.

Did my choice to move on from that early relationship invalidate my career? Were my early concerns about social causes insincere or false simply because they were awakened by a person for whom I had romantic feelings? I don't think so. What I have described is simply the way individuals discover themselves. It is the way cultures do it too!

So this leads to my first argument.

Religion Is Fading as a Natural Evolutionary Phenomenon

We go through all sorts of stages on our way to maturity. Each of those stages impacts the persons we finally become. That does not mean we are obligated to remain stuck at any particular stage. We keep moving.

Religion socializes a people. It gives a people their first reasons to cooperate together. As time passes, however, a society develops other (and in my view, more mature) reasons for community and progress. We are at a juncture in history in which religion no longer unites us. Indeed, for many cultures, religion has become divisive.

Torri Adams did such a magnificent job with her presentation on Buddhism. Do you remember the end of her talk, when she offered Buddhism as a replacement for Western culture's paradigm? I was stunned to hear her say that. I agree with her that Western culture is shattered; however, I don't think Buddhism or any other religion can put it back together. Our oldest connecting cords—the religious ones—are gone forever, so we desperately need new ones. However, trading one antiquated system for another is hardly the answer!

If you want to reflect deeper on what I have just said, read Peter Watson's book *The Modern Mind*. It is a delightful intellectual history of the twentieth century. As you read about the scientific discoveries, political changes, and new inventions made from 1900 to 1999, you will become aware of the radical shift that began in Western culture among a few intellectuals and then steadily oozed into the daily awareness of working men and women. The shift affected all parts of Western culture—including religion. As a result, even the most conservative Christians or Jews now think very differently from the way their ancestors did.

Christians—and I use Christianity as an example because it is the traditional religion of the West—reacted to the changes in Western culture in three different ways:

1. by accommodating to the culture and revising religion to fit it,

2. by ignoring the implications of cultural change, thereby limiting religion's concern to matters of devotion and piety, and

3. by a hostile entrenchment in the thought forms and social constructs of the nineteenth century.

These different responses have created massive internal divisions within the major Christian denominations.

The first response is what we call theological liberalism. It is, regardless of protests to the contrary, the first step of abandoning the faith.

The second response is a psychological delay technique. It avoids the task of thinking through the implications of modern scientific discoveries. (I call this approach a delay because the children of those who embrace it are left to deal with the task their parents avoid.) This is the form of Christianity that has re-created the traditional worship service into a form of entertaining infomercial and has so effectively used mass marketing to promote it.

The third option is the fundamentalist one: It stubbornly ignores (or downright denies) things like continental drift, DNA markers that indicate a common ancestry between the species, neurological evidence for predisposition to homosexuality, concrete proofs for the theories of relativity, the apparent chaos and self-organizing aspects of the subatomic world, and so forth.

The Islamic jihadists are examples of this third option. They feel the same rage that many other religious people experience at the global secular culture. Jihadists recognize the implications of this cultural shift and are determined to resist it.

Christians in our country also realize that a global shift has occurred, and they too are angry. The reason they don't bomb a bank is probably that they have money in the bank! They have shared in the benefits of secular democracy and progressive capitalism. Thus, American Christians feel particularly conflicted; they are loyal both to what is being displaced (their religion) and to that which is taking its place (modern secular society). The hearts of American Christians are invested in their old way of life, just like the jihadists. Their standard of living, however, is based on their connections to the secular state. Therefore, they talk loudly and sometimes angrily, but they vote and act in ways that protects their pocketbooks.

I am not hostile to religion, although religious people often perceived me that way. I did not come to this conference because I wanted to mock anyone. I am not looking for a chance to attack religion. I came here for the same reason that archaeologists dig under cities and that psychologists investigate the layers of the human psyche: I want to understand the roots of human culture. I want to talk to people who still practice religion as a living and functioning system. Future anthropologists will not be able to do that.

Can you imagine what it would be like to travel back in time to interview an astrologer in ancient Babylon or a doctor in seventeenth-century America? A modern astrologer—at least one who has been raised in a modern industrial country—cannot be authentic in the way an ancient Babylonian could be. A modern astrologer has to consciously suppress too much of his or her own education in order to believe and practice astrology.

A seventeenth-century doctor resurrected to practice in twenty-first-century America would be not a doctor at all—he would be a quack! Time has moved on. But think how much we could learn by talking to one of those doctors from the past.

The first president of the United States died because his doctor cut him open to release "bad blood." Washington's doctor basically killed him. Today that doctor would be prosecuted; back then he was probably consoled because he had lost a patient. Human advance made the practice of "blood letting" obsolete. In the same way, human advance is making religion obsolete. As these systems die, we lose knowledge about what it was like to believe in them.

I don't mean this to demean religion. Modern medicine would not be where it is today without the trial and error of those early practitioners, including the ones that practiced blood letting. The early practitioners of medicine brought us to where we are today. Religion has done the same thing. Our art, ethics, political theories, and many other parts of who we are were birthed either by religion or by our opposition to it. I freely acknowledge this and want to learn about how religion accomplished all it has accomplished.

That leads to my second argument.

Humanism Is More Effective Than Religion for Alleviating Human Suffering

This point hits religion hard because it challenges the element of religious work that nearly all human beings appreciate. But religious systems usually ignore the structural realities that create poverty, promote wealth, reward creativity, advance technology, and build up the general infrastructure of society. Religion offers care and redemption for individuals. This concern is usually helpful and deeply appreciated; it is often inadequate, however. Bringing lasting and comprehensive relief to the human family requires new kinds of social structures to support our good intentions. Religion was developed in a much simpler time, so it cannot respond to socially complicated conditions.

For example, the Christian right is full of compassionate and generous people, but it nonetheless appears indifferent to the plight of those without mass transit, health care, or the means to educate themselves. However, because of these missing elements in our social infrastructure, poor people must constantly take massive risks to accept the low-paying jobs they are qualified to do. For example, a poor man in a city without mass transit must buy a car in order to get to his job. His car must pass emissions control for him to keep the car insured. If he gets sick, his job probably won't provide either health coverage or sick pay. That means he must either go to work ill—which many do, including restaurant workers—or fail to go to work at all and perhaps lose his job. Giving a man like this a hot meal or some clothes will let him know that someone cares about him and that is surely to be appreciated. It does not however, provide this man the means to care for himself.

Many wise, kind, and compassionate people in our country, including very religious ones, often fail to see the problems created by a lack of social infrastructure. Their ethic of individual righteousness cannot address the prevailing sources of pain in modern urban life.

I, along with much of the world, admired Mother Teresa for her work among the poor of Calcutta. However, India's poor have been helped a lot more by the new opportunities in the global marketplace than they ever were by the admirable but relatively ineffective soup kitchens and clothes pantries provided by well-intentioned religious people.

Now I'll move on to my third argument.

Religion Is Now a Social Support System Rather Than a Way of Life

Although this may seem like an insult to some, religion is an art more than it is a science. To be more specific, religion is a drama that invites us all to become actors. If we accept its invitation, we read its script and discover what the play is all about. If we decide to act in it, we memorize our lines and audition for a part. However, the play will not take on real life for us unless we pour our hearts into our roles. If we do, the play may profoundly shape our thinking.

A good drama can help us cope with life outside the theater. If it meets our needs and continues to provoke our thoughts and emotions, we will make it an important part of our culture. Such a play's performance will constantly take on new meaning as the decades and centuries roll by. That's why we hear the lines of Macbeth differently than the people in Shakespeare's time heard them. So even art must evolve with the culture.

Of course, some actors fall so deeply in love with drama that they decide to live in the theater. Some of these people may even lose all interest in the outside world. Nonetheless, the world outside continues to evolve. The outside world cannot comply in every respect with the words, concepts, and plot lines of the theater, however wonderful and profound its plays may be.

This is like the relationship between religion and the culture that surrounds it.

Religion stimulates the human brain much the same way other forms of art do. For example, advertisers try to create jingles that will stick in our heads. A jingle must drive home a message that motivates us to action. Therefore, the music of the jingle can be moving, funny, or even irritating. It doesn't matter. If it is a good jingle, we won't be able to get it out of our heads.

Let me give you an example.

I don't smoke. However, I still know that "Winston tastes good like a cigarette should." I know this a full thirty years after that cigarette company removed its commercial from TV! My brain got colonized. A Winston is not foreign to me anymore. Indeed, were I crazy enough to start smoking, I probably would look for a Winston. (Do they still make them?)

Religion uses music, art, and ceremony to move us. This occurs long before we have the capacity to reason. That's why I still love Christmas. I watch the specials on TV every year. I still know the carols. I appreciate Bach and Rachmaninoff even though I do not share the religious senti- ment that moved them to compose. My cultural habits are now deeply entrenched. I don't resent this; however, neither do I feel compelled to follow all the thoughts of my culture to their origin. In other words, I still hum the jingle; I just don't buy the product.

I think the very sound of "spiritual words" help religions colonize people's brains. Just think about how many times in this symposium people have told us that the ideas of their religion do not translate well from their original language. That's why American converts to Bud- dhism tend to use words like "dharma," and "sanga." Jews talk about "Torah" and "shekinah." And just ask a Christian to translate the word "hallelujah." Muslims don't even believe that a translation of the Koran into another language is really a Koran! So the sounds of words—often poetry—become precious and even hypnotic to those who repeat them in their prayers, hymns, and ceremonial occasions. That's the way art works. It is a culturally conditioned artifact that helps create and maintain the culture that produces it.

A Relay Race

Freud pushed us to develop our understanding of the brain and nervous system. However, if we closely examine Freud (who was, as you know, famously hostile to religion), we discover that some of his central ideas probably came from Augustine. Yet Augustine lived fourteen hundred years before Freud! Augustine's *Confessions* may have even been the first Western psychology text.

So what was St. Augustine writing about when he came up with his penetrating insight into human nature? He was reflecting on St. Paul's epistle to the Romans. This is an example of a sort of ideological relay race. It began with St. Paul, moved to St. Augustine, passed on to Freud, and then continued on to the latest breakthrough at Barrows Neurological Center across town.

This relay race, however, has not been a mere passing of a baton. It has been a process that continually challenged, developed, refined, and reshaped the baton that the philosophers, inventors, and artists were passing to one another. So we honor St. Augustine for writing inspiring literature, but we don't have to agree with his religious reasons for writing that literature. We can also honor Freud for his contribution without believing that women have "penis envy" or that people have an "Oedipus complex." The idea—the baton—kept developing. Each person in the relay process used the tools available to him or her to develop it. So when you go far enough into the past, you find that many of the people who initiated relays like the one I just described were religious. That does not mean that a person or culture has to remain religious in order to profit by the ideas they first proposed. Time has moved on.

In the past, religious institutions often attracted a culture's most brilliant people. As these people went about their spiritual duties, they also reflected on the secular areas of life that most intrigued them. For example, Gregor Mendel, who founded the science of genetics, made his discoveries while tending gardens. His gardens were a part of his monastic assignment. Certainly some religious leaders today are as brilliant as Mendel. In our times, however, a religious leader will not be tending a garden—he will be doing fund raising or business administration. The scientifically minded person will not have gone into the ministry in the first place.

Now, at some level, all religious people living in industrial nations will recognize what I am saying to be true. That is why most churches in our country focus on political and social concerns rather than on rebuking witches as their ancestors may have done. If a pastor gets sick, the people in his congregation will ask for prayer, but they'll also take him to see a doctor. The people of a parish now visit a psychiatrist for their bipolar disorder, not an exorcist. They will go to a career counselor for help finding a vocation, not a pastor. The areas of real responsibility for a clergyperson, in other words, are increasingly symbolic and ceremonial. Successful ministers are now either business entrepreneurs (who offer an alternate community to those who do not fit into other kinds of communities) or entertainers. They are rarely teachers or even spiritual leaders now. This is true of both liberal and conservative churches and is a powerful sign that religion, at least as we have known it, is dying.

Lest I seem to be picking on Christians, I have noticed that Buddhists in our country appeal to the secular mind-set too. They tell us that meditation will lower our blood pressure and increase our mental acumen. They offer all sorts of studies to supposedly prove this. Well, sign me up! However, I don't have to believe in Buddhism to meditate. So if I never go to a temple or read Buddhist literature, will meditation make me a Buddhist? No, it won't. Same goes for Yoga, Transcendental Meditation, hypnosis—any and all kinds of mental states and emotional techniques we have learned from religions, which may or may not have therapeutic value. The issue is, as our religions continue to secularize, how can they keep claiming to be the same thing they once were? This is willful self-delusion I think.

Religious people around the world cannot escape the inevitable secularization and globalization that technology has produced. Globalization provokes people to compare their religion with other faiths. Secularization makes people think of their faith as a comfort rather than as something that is objectively true. This is the process that people of all religions are experiencing.

Religious Rage Is a Reaction to the
Imminent Death of Religion

Some religious people cannot adjust to the advance of secularism. Jihadists, for example, simply cannot live in a world where people embrace values and practices that are different from their own. In other words, jihadists cannot handle personal choice. They cannot allow their faith to become one voice among many in the global marketplace of ideas. So jihadists insist that the clock be turned back several centuries to a time that never really existed in the first place.

The trouble is, jihadists cannot even turn back their own clock. The virus of secularism is already in their own souls. We see their rage against the various sources of their own growing doubts. Jihadists—again, of whatever faith—want a theocracy because they are terrified that their religion cannot survive in a climate of science, freedom of inquiry, technological access to knowledge, and powerful entertainment that opens up new ways of living. Jihadists cannot tolerate giving people the responsibility of choosing their own life.

When a secular-minded person like me reacts against religion, this is the religion we react against. We can live with the other reactions to secularism—to the people who reshape their religion to fit modern life. We can even live with the pietistic decision to ignore the hard questions of science. Of course our preference for these moderate forms of faith opens us up to the not altogether unfounded charge that what angers secular people is "real" religion, the sort around which believers actually organize their lives.

Conclusion

Here is the hard truth about religion: It brought us to where we are, but it cannot take us to where we need to go. We appear to be alone in the cosmos. We have no gods to praise or demons to blame. In our short lives as individuals (and perhaps even our relatively short life as a species), we love, create, and pass on to others the things we value. However, there are no vortexes of cosmic power grids, no UFO abductions, no past lives, no energy crystals, and no disembodied spirits. We live for a few years. We learn what we can. We enjoy our love for our family and friends. We suffer heartache and pain. That is life in the real world.

For our ancestors, religion brought meaning and solace. For an increasing number of the world's population, including many people who once wanted to be religious, religion has lost its ancient power to perform. It cannot hold up under the weight of the new global culture.

In short, religion, at least as we have defined and experienced it in the past, is dying. All religious people are grieving its passing. Some are trying to adapt their religion to the modern world, trying to buy it a few more generations. Others are embittered and hostile and are fighting like the men in the Alamo who would rather die (or even kill) than to live in a world without their faith. Thus, religion, which human culture created to give the peace and unity necessary to civilization, has become one of the greatest dangers to civilization. It was our crib; we must not allow it to become our tomb.

JOURNAL NOTES

After listening to Burtrano, I was exhausted. Unlike the other religious leaders here, he refused to categorize his system as a religion. But what could humanism be other than a religion? It creates values for a culture, it proposes meaning for our existence, and it even offers eschatology to cheer us on. What does "progress" mean if not movement toward a distant goal?

Like other religions, humanism has heroes and saints. It has sacred literature. It has icons. It has testimonies, conversions, and apostasies. It has sacred ground and ecstatic experience. It has taboos and totems. It has missionary zeal to convert others. It even has the ability to oppress and persecute. The fact that its proponents fail to see its dark side is of course not unique either. What Christian will own up to the role of his faith in upholding slavery? What Muslim will admit to the near genocide that it sanctioned against the Armenians? Religions can beguile and deceive as well as heal and comfort. Humanism can do all these things too because it is itself a religion.

If humanists claim that categorizing their belief system as a religion is unfair simply because humanism has no god, we reply that Buddhism also has no god. If humanists protest that their system of thought entertains doubt and the possibility of error, I reply that this is true of Hinduism as well. If it be said that humanism acknowledges the art, philosophy, and benevolent deeds of any and all cultures, I respond that a religion like Baha'i does the same.

The fact is, humanism is Western culture's reaction against the rituals and restrictions of Christianity and Judaism. It is a Judaism without a Moses;

a Christianity without a St. Paul. It may retain Jesus as an icon of human goodness if He does not speak of sin, does not attempt to work miracles, and does not attempt to resurrect Himself from the dead. Of course, this "Jesus" starts to look a lot like Socrates, and that is no surprise—ancient Greece is the holy land of humanism. Socrates, Plato, and Aristotle comprise its holy trinity. Its scripture consists of the works of Homer and Vergil, Voltaire and Rousseau, Whitehead and Nietzsche. Its process of canonization is ongoing; what comprises scripture in one generation becomes heresy in the next. However, sacred texts remain, along with preferred methods of interpreting those texts.

Humanists even have a "holy spirit" of sorts. The authors do not merely create their texts; rather, texts are eternally co-created in the moment of literary interaction between the author and the reader. Meaning, then, is a spirit, blowing where it wishes and moving mysteriously from heart to heart, weaving a communion between enlightened souls in every nation and in every generation.

Humanism also has it temples and priests. Indeed, it has a magisterium (a group that decides what should and should not be taught). It has an inquisition (the zealots who enforce the decisions of the magisterium). Like any religion, humanism's system of thought is formidable and often challenging. However, it often lacks the confidence to allow those within its realm to explore other ways of thinking unless they do so according to the careful guidance of its own priests. Students from traditional religious homes who attempt to live their faith while attending our great universities can attest to this creedal imposition. Like other religions, humanism views conversion as a one-way process: admirable when in it moves people into its own camp, detestable when it moves them in the other direction.

When the old Soviet system sent Alexander Solzhenitsyn into exile, Harvard was delighted. It even asked him to give an important address to its student body. However, after the graduate of the Gulag used his address to predict both the imminent doom of the Soviet state and the inevitable collapse of Western secularism, the old prophet suffered exile again, this time at the hands of the American intelligentsia. He was undoubtedly courageous. He was irrepressibly brilliant, but alas, he was a Christian. Furthermore, he was not the acceptable sort of mild-mannered Christian who used Christianity as a personal sedative. He was the sort that had long been declared extinct by Harvard, Yale, and other repositories of humanistic orthodoxy. He was like a living woolly mammoth who had burst out of Siberia and suddenly threatened to make all the textbooks obsolete. Rural Vermont seemed the right place for the dangerous relic. For a brief moment, Solzhenitsyn lit up the world stage with courage and perseverance, and then he slipped quietly into the oblivion of discredited humanist heroes.

A Cultural Parasite

Burtrano is a nice guy. I would love discussing the philosopy of Prost with him over tea and croissants. However, I would imagine things might heat up a bit if our conversation turned to cultural source material. There the truth might become obvious: Humanism is a cultural parasite. Generation after generation, it feeds from the thought, behavior, and emotion of believers. Whether with praise or blame, humanism is always reacting to the Old and the New Testaments. What is Voltaire without French Catholicism? What is Rousseau without a garden of Eden and a primal state of innocence? How does one separate a Martin Luther King from his Bible or a B.F. Skinner from his childhood Calvinism? Our textbooks must labor to obscure the roots of their heroes, lest the fruit of their work somehow be traced to the emotions and ideals that formed their infancy.

I do not mean to deny that humanism has a certain power and beauty. How could a Christian, believing as he does that human beings embody the image and likeness of God, refuse to acknowledge the glory and grace that all men and women reflect? I claim only that humanism is not always objective or inevitably honest. Humanism's stance toward Christians often reminds me of Christians who hate Jews, as though our faith were even possible without the genius and transcendent glory of ancient Jerusalem.

Burtrano thinks that Bach is possible without a Bible. However, what does he think *Jesu Joy of Man's Desiring* could possibly mean without a Jesu? How do we get a Dante or a Milton without Genesis or the mass? In all that humanism seems to admire in Western culture, we find artifacts created by a people who were either in love with God or boiling in hatred against Him. And just as humanism seemed to finally enter an age free of Christianity, just when humanism appeared finally to be developing its own path without reference to religion, the other world religions suddenly reasserted themselves.

I can't think of a single era in a single nation when humanism has existed as a stand-alone entity. Even in ancient Greece and Rome, humanism fed itself from the fruit of paganism. Humanists could smile indulgently at the ancient gods and goddess, but they used them to allegorize their principles.

Marcus Aurelius, the humanist emperor, famously wanted to be free of the Galilean. However, he knew that his Christless state required a revival of Jupiter and Aphrodite. Even Aurelius seemed not to have considered the possibility of a state without gods or a culture without myth. Burtrano says that religion is dead. I say that humanism is dead.

What About Orthodoxy?

Burtrano makes the common mistake of acknowledging only one form of biblical fidelity: fundamentalism. He sees two other Christian reactions to secularism, namely mainline liberalism and pietistic evangelicalism. Christian liberalism he sees as a recreation of Christianity, an attempt to avoid its own utter destruction from the inevitable advance of science. Evangelicalism he sees as a retreat from culture into a form of religious romanticism. He says this will buy socially conservative Christians perhaps another generation to practice their faith in peace. Fundamentalism is the only real religion for Burtrano, the only one he fears has the power to sway the masses away from science.

Burtrano fails to acknowledge the other alternative to secularism: Christian orthodoxy. I do not use the term "orthodox" to refer merely to those churches who call themselves "Orthodox." By "orthodoxy," I mean all believers in Christ who hold fast to that which has at all times and in all places been believed by the whole people of God.[1] Orthodoxy includes great intellectuals, people like Augustine and Aquinas, who were neither afraid to disagree with their adversaries nor to borrow from them to broaden their own understanding. Aquinas wrestled with the newly rediscovered Aristotle; he did not burn the philosopher's books while singing hymns. Jonathan Edwards did a lot more than preach about "Sinners in the Hands of an Angry God"; he studied Sir Isaac Newton's discoveries and expanded his understanding of God's creation. These men did not hide from the world's growing knowledge. They did not retreat into mere privatistic devotion; they engaged with life while remaining committed to their faith.

Ignoring continental drift, quantum mechanics, and the theories of relativity is not fidelity to God; it is fear masquerading as piety. Orthodoxy does not empower such fear. Like humanism, orthodoxy looks at all parts of life, but it looks at it through a very different lens. Humanism denies that it looks through any lens of course, believing as it does in the immaculate perception. Its blindness is as incurable as that of the most wild-eyed religious fanatic.

Humanistic Coercion

Humanists rightfully recognize that conservative religious people can get angry and even become violent against secularization. But humanists do not always realize how the violence can run the other way. They do not realize this because they see themselves as being always on the side of reason, science, progress, and liberation. However, secular tolerance for religious people is not nearly as great as secularists would like us to believe.

For example, when humanists think of the children of a religious community—the Amish, for example—they cannot help but feel sorry for them. "Poor children! Growing up like that, without lightbulbs and computers," they say, shaking their heads. And sometimes their sorrow turns to anger. "What parents would do such a terrible thing to their children?" they ask. "This is abuse! It has to be stopped." But of course, the Amish parents are raising their children as they do because they want to give their children their most precious possession—their faith. Amish parents don't want to join the modern workforce, put their children in daycare, or raise them in front of a television. They would rather work the farm with their children. They just can't seem to view this as abuse.

Humanists claim the right to decide. As the sole judge of truth, they have the right and responsibility to decide.

I do agree with Burtrano on one thing: Fundamentalism is indeed based on primal fear, the fear that one's group and its values will become extinct if global secularization continues. However, secular people are capable of feeling the same sort of fear. Consider how they react when religious people try to participate in government—I mean when religious people try to govern from their own core values rather than those cherished by secular people. Secular people fear that if religious people get control of government, liberty will be endangered. The unavoidable but sad truth is that the fears of both the traditional believer and the secular person are probably well-founded. Fundamentalists and humanists probably can't coexist.

Whether humanist or Christian fundamentalist, a fanatic is a fanatic. If people cannot discern between private loyalty and public coercion, they cannot live in peace with those who differ.

The reason Alexander Solzhenitsyn was such an embarrassment at Harvard was that his resistance to the old Soviet Union, however noble, was motivated by entirely wrong ideas. He deplored the godlessness of the atheistic state and did not view the godlessness of the West as a viable alternative. His presence at Harvard revealed that however much at odds

American humanists were with the brutality of the Soviet State, they shared the politburo's opinions about the inevitable death of religion. Our universities do not torture religious people or put them in prison, but they often do make sure that those who take their religion seriously do not remain in places of influence. Solzhenitsyn had to be stopped.

Humanism retains the right to tell the story of culture and to interpret it as it pleases. It still claims to be the sole judge of truth.

For example, humanists often tell us that history's most bloody regimes were based on religion. That has been said so often now that we tend to casually accept the statement as irrefutable. But it is simply not accurate. Stalin was not religious—unless Communism is a religion. Hitler was not religious—unless National Socialism was a religion. Mao Tse-Tung was not religious. Yet these three men slaughtered multiplied millions of people, all in the name of establishing states without gods or devils. The three men might not have been humanists, but they were undoubtedly secular.

Religious people are not more inclined to cruelty than others; they just have less excuse. The ones with the least excuse are those who believe that "all have sinned and fall short of the glory of God."[2] People who believe that must never persecute and must not coerce.

Summary

Humanism is a stepchild of the Judeo-Christian West. It came from an ancient stream of culture that continued to flow through the West after the defeat of paganism and the death of the classical Greek philosophers. Through the centuries, it has absorbed many of the values of its Christian environment, but it remains an alternate way of viewing the world. As Christianity lost its power to lead Western culture, humanism emerged for a brief moment to assert its legitimacy as the West's authentic voice. However, its power is already waning. Humanism's children chose not to accept its values. The culture has thus decided for the moment to leave the core of the Western world empty and without form, disdaining its own historical values but not yet ready to replace them.

It is tempting to view the state of Western culture through the words of Genesis 1:2, which tells us that our entire universe was once in the same shape Western civilization is today: "without form, and void." Just before creation, "Darkness was on the face of the deep." But "the Spirit of God was hovering over the face of the waters."

May it be so with our own fractured and diseased culture. Right now it is deeply at odds with Moses and Christ. However, the West is still a repository for much that is worth redeeming and that still often reflects the glory of the Lord.

Humanists often value things that Christians have forgotten. One wonders if Christians, on their own, would still appreciate the works of Bach, Tolstoy, Hugo, and Milton. Even though the humanists often interpret these works in ways that we cannot affirm, they at least honor them, which is more than what many Christians care to do. Perhaps if we were still giving things of such great value to our culture instead of merely criticizing it, we might find that some humanists are merely people who care about culture. Perhaps many humanists still hope to find in some artifact of our culture a quality that is not of this world and that points the way to the world to come.

In that case, the burden of responsibility is upon the people of God to write, paint, sing, dance, speak, heal, research, and create so that those who cannot yet accept our message will nonetheless accept our gifts. If so, our gifts can become once more, as they often have been through the centuries, a cup of water to those who are thirsty.

the people
of covenant:
judaism and the way of the book

The fear of the LORD is the beginning of knowledge.

PROVERBS 1:7

D r. Rebecca Aaronson was not what you call a chatty person. I found that out at the coffeepot at the back of the room. I had tried to strike up a conversation with her while I added cream to my coffee. She didn't seem very interested in talking—at least not then.

I felt a little rebuffed by her reserved manner. So I didn't try to talk to her during lunch later in the day.

Momentary impressions can fasten themselves to our minds. We can form judgments so quickly and yet defend those superficial impressions so passionately. This is a quirk of human nature that requires a good deal of maturity to overcome. But overcome we must, especially when our judgments are about personalities and customs that merely stretch our sense of comfort.

I have discovered that a person I like at first may simply know how to make a good impression. Good salespeople know how to be liked regardless of whether they have character or competence. Besides, being nice is not the same as being good. Likewise, being gruff is not always an indication of bad character. We have to work to embrace truth from those who are not socially adept and reject falsehood from those who are merely fun to be with.

Dr. Aaronson did not seem particularly fun to be with. So I had to resist the impulse to close my mind to her words.

That is the way contemporary people often judge biblical faith. Paganism seems so much more fun. My imagination can go wild playing with images of frolic and freedom, release from all responsibilities, running naked through the woods chasing a nymph. (Okay, I'm sorry about the nymph, but you get the idea.) How can you compare such delightful images with "thou shalt not"?

My immediate response to a "thou shalt not" tends to be, "Well, why shouldn't I? My inner child wants it! Who are you to tell me that I can't have it, can't do it, and can't think about it?"

Franz Rosenzweig, a Jewish theologian who wrote in the early years of the twentieth century, claimed in *The Star of Redemption* that to remain spiritually healthy, Christianity needs a vibrant Judaism. He said that Jews are a constant impediment to our natural tendency to slide back into paganism.

In other words, we need a "thou shalt not."

Ouch!

St. Paul called the Torah, or Hebrew teaching, a "schoolmaster."[1] Same idea, I guess.

Well, Dr. Aaronson struck me as a schoolmaster. I thought she might take my gum if I chomped on it during class. I pictured her sending me to the principal's office for passing notes.

How unfair my imagination was to Dr. Aaronson! She actually had been kind enough to take time off work and come here each day to listen and to discuss religion with the rest of us.

As she was walking to the podium, I decided she was probably in her early sixties. Her hair was pulled back in a tight knot of some sort and was mostly pearl white except for some dark stands that I thought revealed its original color. The hair combined with her chiseled features and olive skin to create an impression of elegance and nobility. She wore small silver earrings that looked like strands of tiny rope, but the only other piece of jewelry was the tiny silver star of David hanging around her neck.

Good afternoon.

Her accent reminded me of New York for some reason. However, the accent was not quite like that of other New Yorkers I had known. I heard something else, some lilt in her words that I couldn't quite place.

Well, no time for that; she was already plunging into her topic.

The differences between Judaism and the other world religions are vast. Christianity and Islam profess historical connections with Judaism, so it is in the interests of those religions to maintain continuity with our prophets and with our Scriptures. Nonetheless, our differences even with these other two monotheistic faiths are serious enough that we remain a separate people, exasperatingly so to both religions. Our difference with other world religions is even more pronounced and profound.

Jews Are a Separate and a Distinct People

From the moment when God called Abraham out of Ur to this present day, Jews have been a living symbol of difference and distinction. The very existence of these people has been the private obsession of more than one tyrant. What does one do, after all, with a people who choose to burn rather than to bend?

King Nebuchadnezzar, who ruled a vast empire from the ancient city of Babylon, was neither the first nor the last to put Hebrew resilience to the test. Three young Hebrews, who otherwise served their king faithfully and dutifully, astounded Nebuchadnezzar by their refusal to bow before his likeness. They preferred to walk into a fiery oven, which had probably been prepared to frighten the king's subjects into submission.

From Nebuchadnezzar to Hitler, rulers and states have pondered what to do with a people who are loyal citizens but who reserve an even greater loyalty to some principle or entity that emperors and potentates find difficult to understand.

Their God is invisible. They disappear from society once a week. They argue and debate their entire lives about a tradition of thought that boasts as many layers as centuries have passed since Moses. They represent a fraction of the world's population and yet routinely achieve distinction in the arts, sciences, and commerce.

This last fact provoked centuries of violent European reaction. The most persistent theory was that Jews worked in a vast conspiratorial web. It was probably best refuted by Rabbi Daniel Lapin in his book *Thou Shall Prosper.* He countered that Jews didn't get along well enough with one another to create a conspiracy!

Jews are certainly not a monolithic community. Many Jews live secular rather than religious lives. Those who are religious congregate within three major branches of their faith: Orthodox, Conservative, and Reform. Some Jewish communities have a mystical orientation, such as

the people of covenant

the Hasidim. Some communities are related to ethnicity and cultural influences, like the Ashkenazim and the Sephardim, who represent respectively the northern and southern strands of European Jewish life. Other groups of Jews stretch from the Falasha in Ethiopia to the Cochin Jews in India. Differences of language exist as well, from Yiddish, a linguistic child of Hebrew and German, to Ladino, the offspring of Spanish and Hebrew, to Malayalam, a Hebrew-influenced derivative of Sanskrit.

Whether all these differences will survive, now that Hebrew is once again spoken as Israel's national language, is a real question. However, the differences will likely remain between observant and nonobservant Jews and between the various manners in which the observance is practiced.

Yet despite these differences, the world still reacts to the word "Jew." It is usually a matter of indifference whether the Jew in question is a Communist or a Republican, Sephardic or Ashkenazic, or whether he or she does or does not eat shellfish. The word "Jew" is enough to mark this people known for their difference and distinction.

For our purposes here today, I would like to accept and expand upon this perception—as overblown and prejudicial as it can be.

Generation after generation, country after country, and century after century, Jews have reflected on the words of Torah and have developed unique ways of looking at things.

Here are some of the central beliefs that have molded our ways of looking at life:

1. There is but one God who created and who rules all things.

2. Time is linear. It had a beginning, and it will have an ending.

3. History gradually moves toward an ultimate purpose.

4. Human beings are made in God's image and likeness.

5. God has given us the Torah to make us a witness to all nations.

6. God has called out the Jewish people to demonstrate His love and His sovereignty through a special arrangement called "covenant."

Let's begin with worldview. That is where we encounter the most serious and fundamental differences between Hebrew thought and that of all other ancient cultures. Most of the religions of Asia, for example, treat time and matter as illusionary or at least as lesser realms. Thus, the religious practices of these religions aim at transcending one's sense of time and space. In these religions, a human being is thought to be trapped within an identity limited by space and time. In such a belief system, one is never at home in a material body or in a material world.

In contrast, for the Jew, the material universe is a God-appointed realm within which we are privileged to live, love, and glorify God. We are material creatures not because of a curse but because of God's good purpose. Therefore, we learn to live joyfully within the boundaries of time and matter—in much the same way as a person lives between the borders of his or her native land. For this reason, Jews do not attempt to escape the material world, either by denying its reality or by purposefully entering into shamanistic states of consciousness. Indeed, such practices are forbidden for us (although some aberrant groups within Judaism seem not to agree with the prohibition).

Jews Relate to God as Family

Jews are called to live their lives trusting in the sovereignty of their Creator. This trust includes the right to question God and even to feel frustrated with His actions or with His lack of action. But it never includes the right to disobey Him.

A story from the Nazi death camps illustrates what I mean. A rabbi was with a group of Jews one day when, to their horror, a young man broke into a run toward the electric fence and grabbed it with both hands. He was immediately electrocuted before their very eyes. After a few moments of silence, the rabbi said, "That's it. I don't believe in God!"

The Jews were astounded and perplexed. "Rabbi," they said, "you mustn't say such a thing!"

"But it's true," the old man repeated. "I don't believe in God."

As they stood around, plunging deeper and deeper into their grief, the old rabbi began walking toward the barracks.

"Where are you going, Rabbi?" one of the men asked.

"It's time for prayer," he replied.

"But Rabbi, you just said that you don't believe in God anymore!" the man responded.

At this the old rabbi threw his hands into the air and said with a sense of exasperation, "I know I don't believe in God, but it's time for prayer!"

Of course the old rabbi had not really denounced his faith. He was just hurt and bewildered. However, as a son of Abraham, he is a part of a tradition that argues with the Creator as well as worships Him. God is family. Once the rabbi had gotten his anger off his chest, it was time to pray. Family life must go on.

Abraham Joshua Heschel once pointed out that although the ancient Hebrews would not have objected that their God was the "prime mover unmoved," or the "first cause," as the Greek philosophers taught, no Hebrew would have used such language. A Hebrew described God in relational rather than in philosophical terms. To a Jew, the Creator is "the God of Abraham, Isaac, and Jacob." This sense of relationship with God is the core of Jewish faith.

Even Jews whose lives have not been marked by religious observance will often recite the Shema in their moments of mortal danger: *Sh'ma Yis'ra'eil Adonai Eloheinu Adonai echad.* (Hear, O Israel: The Lord our God, the Lord is one.)

The words are at the core of our being. They connect us to one another and to the one who called us to be a people. So our faith is about relationship to God. People from many religions might say the same thing. However, the Jewish relationship with God is so intimate that it includes the right to appeal as well as the responsibility to submit. Abraham argued with God. Moses argued with God. The psalmists argued with God.

God has asked us to be His family, and families are not all sweetness and light! So sometimes we argue with one another in our family, and that includes God.

Perhaps I am making too much of the Jewish inclination to argue with the Almighty. However, this feature of Jewish piety is at the core of how we differ from other religions. It means that God is not an abstraction to us. He, like us, is a relational being.

The God of Abraham, Isaac, and Jacob created all things. However, God gave the things He created the freedom to exist independently—or even rebelliously.

Our ancient stories tell how the quest for absolute freedom deceived humanity's ancestors and led them to abandon their knowledge of God. That's how the natural ways of humankind became dark and twisted. As a result, human beings became naturally inclined to move toward an utter dependence on God and one another on one hand, or toward anarchy on the other.

That is why God called Abraham out from Ur. Ur represents the natural state of humankind, where freedom is misused or lost altogether. God wanted to reveal a new way of living to Abraham, one that the natural order could not offer. God wanted to teach Abraham how to form a family and community around law and justice.

The essence of the Torah—God's written instructions—is about how to live above and beyond a state of pure nature. (As an aside, Leon Kass has just written a most wonderful book about this topic called *The Beginning of Wisdom*. If you want to know more about how Jews understand the world and the Bible, pick up that book!)

The story of how God called Abraham out from the natural order is repeated with many other biblical people. Each of the patriarchs wrestled with his difference and distinction and made a decision about whether he would choose God's way over the natural way. Jacob did it after having lived a life of deceit and having become Israel. Joseph did it despite his family's betrayal of him. He then struggled about whether he would be an Egyptian or a Hebrew. Even David had to decide whether to become a warlord among the Philistines or a hunted man among the Israelites. Esther had to decide whether to be first the queen of an empire or first the niece of an out-of-favor Jew.

All of these people were "called out," put on the spot, and forced to choose and declare their ultimate loyalties. So are we all. Sooner or later we all must choose our ultimate loyalties.

The one story that overshadows all the rest is the one we tell once a year at Passover. That is the night we acknowledge our difference and distinction from others. A young child asks the same question each year: "Why is this night unlike every other night?"

The answer reminds us that this night is different because the people who ask the question are different. "Because this is the night that God delivered us out of the hand of Pharaoh."

We remember that our people were slaves in of Egypt. However, when God was ready, he sent Moses to lead His people back to their own land. This is why we gather once a year for Passover—so we can rehearse with our families what God said that night to our ancestors. We recall what God did for us on the night when He led us out from the house of bondage. We are a people who remember who we are and whose we are. We have often gone the wrong way, but we do not stay lost because we know the way home. That's why it is a rare thing indeed—even for non-religious Jews—not to observe Passover.

While God's people were on the Exodus journey, on another night that would reorder heaven and earth, God gave Moses the gift of all gifts—the Torah. God promised the slaves that if they would accept the Torah—if they would study it diligently through all their generations—God would make them a people unlike any other.

Jewish Practices

A good way to understand how Jews live and practice their faith is to read Herman Wouk's book *This Is My God*. It has been around for a generation, so some of its issues now seem provincial and outdated. Nonetheless, it is still a delightful and informative book.

Perhaps the first thing to learn about Jewish practice is this: Once a week, Jews leave their day-to-day lives and experience sacred time.

The Jewish philosopher Abraham Joshua Heschel poetically said that we Jews build our cathedral in time rather than in space. What he meant was that Jews require a set-apart time for worship more than they need a set-apart space.

During this holy time called Sabbath, we hear the words of God. We invite those words into our lives. Some Jews have had ecstatic experiences at such times. However, this is not the norm and is not particularly encouraged. Sabbath is about encountering holiness in order to gain the wisdom and courage we need to carry out our responsibilities. Sabbath helps us live out our faith, in other words, within a material world and within a human culture.

The implication of our this-worldly faith is that any renunciation of family responsibilities, the neglect for one's body, or even the forsaking of one's financial resources cannot be a legitimate expression of piety. The Creator made human beings to live interconnectedly. Spirituality is thus about becoming mutually responsible toward one another. Therefore, the heart of our faith is about maintaining our obligations to God and to the people of God.

This is the meaning of the word "covenant," an acceptance of holy obligations and relationships. Our ancestors made contracts with God that govern our lives. To be a Jew is to accept these obligations, generation after generation.

A Jew thus is a trustee, a steward of all the resources within his or her control. This stewardship is carried out on behalf of our ancestors of course. However, perhaps more importantly, this stewardship is exercised on behalf of our descendents. In other words, I cannot "own" my wealth. Rather, I am a trustee of resources that move through me from others and to others. The same principle governs the invisible resources of our lives as well—things such as faith and covenant.

On the seventh day, God commands me to leave all I have been doing on the other days. On that day, I rest and reflect. When I return to my daily work, I remember how it fits within the larger picture of my life. I pay greater attention to how the work affects the life of my community and the lives of those who will come after me.

We are material creatures who live within time and space. Therefore we must trust, obey, and learn from the God who created us. We are not God, and we cannot become God. This is another way in which we differ from many other religions: We are content to be fully mortal.

In fact, the first story of the Torah is about how human beings made a tragic decision to ignore the differences between them and their Creator. The result was poverty, sickness, and death. We need reminders of God's otherness and of our human limits so we will not repeat the mistake of forgetting our mortality.

The Sabbath is like the tree in the middle of the garden of Eden. It is holy because God says it is holy. All other parts of creation God declared "good"; the Sabbath He pronounced "holy," or "other."

Why?

We are not sure. It is enough that God says that if we will treat this day differently, we will become a different kind of people. This is how Abraham Heschel put it:

> The Seventh day is an armistice in man's cruel struggle for existence, a truce in all conflicts, personal and social, peace between man and man, man and nature, peace within man; a day on which handling money is considered a desecration, on which man avows his independence of that which is the world's chief idol.
>
> The seventh day is the exodus from tension, the liberation of man from his own muddiness, the installation of man as a sovereign in the world of time.[2]

As I have been saying—and perhaps now wearing upon your patience—the Bible emphasizes the spiritual importance of difference and distinction. The opening pages of the Bible tell us that night is not day, men are not women, human beings are not God, and the seventh day is unlike the other six. The theme is preparing us for the moment when God will call Abraham out from Ur. He will separate Abraham from all other men so he can become a different sort of father to a different sort of people.

We acknowledge this difference and distinction when our boys first come into the world. Jewish families immediately arrange for boys' circumcision as a permanent sign of difference that they can never erase. It tells the child that he, and all who will be born to him, are set apart. A Jew is Abraham's child. A Jew is a father or a mother to Abraham's children. Each generation thus becomes a channel through which God's covenant to Abraham will flow from one age into the next. That responsibility takes precedence over all others, whether private or public.

All things intimately related to life carry some sign to remind Jews of their covenant. Circumcision does this. The Sabbath does it. Dietary restrictions do it too.

So Jews must not eat some things. Like the tree in Eden, these are off limits—they are "other." Sometimes this seems to make sense; pork, after all, is a dangerous source of food in a world without refrigeration. However, sometimes, as with that famous fruit in the garden, the prohibition seems to have no logic. It is enough to say, "Jews do not eat this."

We call such prohibitions "mitzvoth." They reflect and cultivate our faith. Our hearts are often ignorant; they must be instructed. Our understanding is faulty; it must be tutored. Mitzvoth force reflection and foster humility. They open the possibility to become God conscious and covenant centered.

When we eat Passover, we ask, "Why on other nights do we eat bread with yeast, but on this night we do not eat yeast?" The answer is not that yeast is an inherently evil substance; it is that a different taste provokes a question that would have otherwise gone unasked. Unleavened bread jars us into asking a different question.

Why can I not conduct a business deal on the Sabbath? Because one day of the week I must acknowledge that business deals are not the essence of my existence.

Why do I not eat dairy products and meat at the same time? Because even though I may kill an animal to eat it, I must not become cruel or mindless to suffering—even of the animals I eat. The prohibition against mixing dairy and meat comes from a Bible passage that forbids the use of cow's milk to cook her calf. Like blood, milk is meant to sustain life. It must be treated in ways that acknowledge our gratitude for life. Eating kosher is a way of expressing our respect and gratitude to God for our food and compassion to the animals God created for our use. Cruel means of butchering thus make meat unfit for Jews. We refuse to profit from suffering. That is why we must remind ourselves to abhor all forms of cruelty.

Can all of these rules become routine, a system of monotonous, pointless loyalty to an antiquated system of thought? Of course. A mitzvah cannot teach us if we refuse to learn from it. So the performance of a mitzvah does not guarantee we will automatically become better people. Nonetheless, our code of life will teach us if we decide to pay attention to its lessons.

My grandson is learning his multiplication tables now. His mother makes him repeat them every night after dinner. The other night he said to me, "Grandma, why do I have to say all these numbers? It is so boring!"

I told him it was so he could take care of my money when I get too old to remember how to do it for myself!

He looked at me like I was as out of it as his parents!

It is not easy for him to see the connection between memorizing the multiplication tables and taking care of his grandmother. The multiplication tables do not create money. They do not build bridges. However, adults know that the multiplication tables create an infrastructure of numbers, and that makes economy, engineering, and other disciplines possible.

A mitzvah makes goodness possible. It trains us to become aware of our actions and to gradually mold our lives by God's teachings. Heschel described the process this way: "God is hiding in the world. Our task is to let the divine energy emerge from our deeds."[3]

Judaism, then, is a this-worldly religion, one of deeds rather than thoughts, one of time rather than space, one of relationships rather than abstractions. Our spirituality emphasizes difference and distinction rather than sameness and underlying unity. All of this points to the single aim of becoming responsible people.

The emergence of personhood is essential if we are to become capable of making meaningful relationships. A person, even a godly person, is different and distinct from other persons. Thus, Moses is a different man from Abraham but not a lesser one. David is not Solomon, and Aaron is not Isaiah. And yet the differences between these leaders were as essential to their importance as were their commonalities. God is the God of Abraham, Isaac, and Jacob. They were different men, relating in different ways to one another and to God.

The prophet Nathan rebukes David the king but does not lose his head because of it. This is because Nathan has a different place in the nation than the king has. It is not a lesser one, however. Both David and Nathan are subjects of God before they are subjects of a state. This is the great irritant of Jewish attitude toward nations and governments—that no person is lesser than another, whatever his or her social station.

There is but one God. The state is not God. Man is not God. Money is not God. Race is not God. Language is not God. Only God is God. Human beings must bow to no one and to nothing but Him. This belief infers the equality of human beings as well as the sovereignty of God.

That is what Judaism offers to humanity: the knowledge that we are all made in God's image and likeness and that we maintain our dignity by submitting to no one but to the one who created us. That is why we can sum up the teachings of our faith as follows: We love God with our whole heart, mind, and strength, and because we do, we love our neighbors as ourselves.

JOURNAL NOTES

Christian attitudes about Judaism have ranged from persecution to outright veneration. In some centuries, Christian leaders have discouraged the study of Hebrew, insisting that the Greek version of the Old Testament should be preferred over the Hebrew original. In contrast, many American evangelicals now come precariously close to acknowledging two paths to salvation—one for Jews and another for Gentiles.

The reason for this Christian confusion about Judaism is simple: We cannot refute it as we do other religions. When a Christian refutes Judaism, he is like a man who works on the third floor but decides to blow up the first story of the same building because he doesn't like the people who work down there. At the same time, The New Testament asserts that Christ is is the Savior of all, Jew and Gentile. It also tells us that God has removed "the middle wall of separation," or the barrier that once separated Jews and Gentiles, and Gentiles have been made "fellow citizens with the saints and members of the household of God."[4] Now, "those who are of faith are sons of Abraham…those who are of faith are blessed with Abraham…there is neither Jew nor Greek."[5] Passages like these abound in the New Testament. They make it impossible for a Christian to either eliminate the notion of Jews as the people of God or to think of them as somehow having a separate relationship to God apart from us. The New Testament teaches that any kind of person who makes the same step of faith that Abraham made is a Jew, so being a Jew is no longer about race.

And yet, St. Paul admonishes us to honor the physical descendents of Abraham. "To them pertain the covenants…and the promises"[6] he says. He asks us to bless them and to treat them tenderly.

Pardon us if we get a bit confused!

We do well to look at modern Judaism as something other than merely the faith of the Old Testament. Modern Judaism has, to be sure, a historical connection and continuity with the faith of the ancient Hebrews. However, its relationship to the ancient faith is not a more legitimate one than that of Christianity. Nor is it less. Viewed in this way, modern Christianity and Judaism are more like siblings than like parent and child.

As with many siblings, the greatest struggles between Jew and Christian have been about legitimacy and inheritance. The ancient Hebrew faith had two children. (Muslims claim that it had three.) Each faith then lays claim to common roots.

The New Testament explanation for how Jew and Christian relate goes back to the Old Testament prophets. The prophets taught that although all of the people of Israel were blessed simply by being a part of the nation, only a small group of Abraham's children had real spiritual understanding. The rest were merely going through the motions. The prophets called that small group, those Jews who had spiritual understanding, "the remnant."[7]

The prophets claimed that God would make a new covenant with this remnant. It would be like a stump of a tree that had been cut down but that had blossomed to grow again.[8] God would then invite other nations to join this Jewish remnant in making a covenant with God. St. Stephen was stoned for claiming that the prophecies about the remnant and the gathering of the Gentiles was taking place in his generation.[9] St. James, at the Council of Circumcision, came to the same conclusion.[10] Thus, the

New Testament writers not only insisted that they were Jews but also that they were that remnant that God would use to invite other nations into the Jewish covenant.

This was the flashpoint that brought division between Jews and Christians. St. Luke tells us in the book of Acts that believers were first called Christians at Antioch. That was not a coincidence; Antioch was the city where non-Jews were deliberately added to the church in large numbers. Furthermore, these new converts were not required to undergo circumcision or to observe Jewish dietary restrictions.

To the Jews, the Nazarenes in Antioch (Christians) had crossed the line. Therefore, they could no longer be viewed as Jews. To the Christians however, the church at Antioch was a miracle, a fulfillment of the words of the prophets. Gentiles were now following the God of Abraham, Isaac, and Jacob, and thus, the very definition of "Jew" had expanded.

By the time the New Testament era was over, maintaining unity between these very different perspectives had become impossible.

As the centuries passed, ethnic Jewish believers became a shrinking minority within the church. Finally, they were even persecuted because of their often conflicted views on the divinity of Jesus. (Some scholars, Hans Kung among them, believe that Jewish forms of Christianity heavily influenced the rise of Islam. However, that is a huge discussion for another place!)

The anger and bitterness of this first-century division has deeply affected Jewish and Christian relationships since. The contention has been about legitimacy: Jews could not accept Christians as members of the same covenant; Christians could not accept the continuity of Judaism separate from the church.

We should acknowledge the political elements in the struggle between the religions, whatever theological position we take. The Jewish leaders in Jerusalem were not about to endanger their precarious peace with the Romans by allowing the spread of any sort of religious fervor that might flame into an insurrection. They knew—and history shows that they were correct—that the Romans would brutally crush any revolt, leaving Jerusalem in ruins. However, the painful experience of being cast out of the synagogue (as the Gospels put it) left a bitter taste in the mouths of Christians. Therefore, when it came their time to be in power, Christians proved themselves to be as capable of persecuting Jews as the old Jewish guard in Jerusalem had been of persecuting Christians.

The history of our relationship does include some bright spots. Early

Christians accepted the ruling of the Jewish elders in Jamnia (AD 90) on the Old Testament canon. By doing so, Christians acknowledged that God might still speak to the guardians of the covenants and promises. Pope Paul, at the death of Abraham Joshua Heschel, called him his favorite theologian. However, such acknowledgments of mutual respect for our common heritage and for one another have been far too few.

It is perhaps guilt for the role of Christian Europe in the slaughter of Jews that moved many evangelical believers to become such fervent advocates of the State of Israel. We have become determined that on our watch there will be no more holocausts, no more burning of synagogues, no more dishonoring of David's star. If our theological explanations for this newfound zeal for our Hebrew heritage is shaky (and it often is), our motivation is usually sincere. It seems untrustworthy to many Jews because it has come so late in history. However, even though we can surely find a better foundation than Christian Zionism upon which to build an appreciation for Jews, it is a start. It is a far better approach than what we have tried before!

For many reasons, disagreeing with Jews has become emotionally difficult for evangelicals. One of the reasons that I mentioned already is that St. Paul told us to treat the Jews tenderly (although he did not always heed his own advice). Another reason is that we feel that our sins against the Jews have been so grievous that we have lost our right to critique their religion. Yet another reason for remaining silent around Jews is that we often feel like younger brothers and sisters when disagreeing with Judaism.

None of these are legitimate reasons for not critiquing Jewish thought. Jewish culture encourages debate, and we, as well as they, are the better for it. Dr. Aaronson said that a Jewish relationship with God involves argument. She said that God doesn't get angry and go away just because we do not understand why He does what He does. That means that we can voice our disagreements with those with whom we are in relationship. This is surely true about our relationships with Jews. When we are respectful, when we honor them as people as well as because they represent the roots of our faith, we should feel free to express our belief that Jesus Christ is the embodiment of Torah as well as the Son of David.

Of course, we must be prepared for their response. They have reasons for not believing in Jesus as Son of God. For us to listen respectfully to their arguments is not blasphemy. If we listen, we may gain an invitation to share our understanding of Scripture, Jesus, and the law. We may also learn something!

As we have seen, St. Paul tells us that the Torah was like a schoolmaster, a tutor appointed by a loving Father to bring us to maturity. The Ten Commandments—or, as Jewish people call them, the Ten Words—begin with a declaration of divine authority. "I am the Lord your God, who brought you out of the land of Egypt, out of the house of bondage." Only after this declaration do the Ten Words instruct us about how to live. This schoolmaster claims the right to speak!

In our times, we are usually guilty of skipping school. No schoolmaster for us. We are moving on to grace. In the past, however, our ancestors often erred in the other way—staying in grammar school, repeating the Ten Commandments and the moral code, proclaiming the foundations of ethics and morals until their spiritual life was nearly drained of joy.

So we revolted against the schoolmaster. We decided not to study. We decided that rules had no role in our lives. We would worship and celebrate. No structure of worship for us with its prayers of repentance and its affirmations of forgiveness. No repetition of the Ten Commandments followed with a plea to God, "Lord, have mercy upon us, and incline our hearts to keep this law."[11] School was out. We were enjoying summer vacation—forever.

Some American evangelical groups even began to call the Hebrew Scriptures "the Old Bible," as if the Old Testament had somehow been made obsolete by the New. That was a far cry from the affirmation many of us pastors made at ordination, that "we believe the Old and the New Testaments to be the veritable Word of God and to contain all things necessary for salvation." That vow should have prevented us from reducing two-thirds of the Holy Scripture to "the Old Bible." Unfortunately it didn't. So our theology suffered accordingly.

The Anglican Mission to the Americas recently released a statement that beautifully expresses the relationship between the Old and New Testaments. Carefully reviewing the words and reflecting on their meaning is worth our time:

> With regard to the interpretation of Holy Scripture, we affirm the clarity of its plain sense so that it may and can be understood by ordinary readers. We hold to the importance of the scholarly interpretation of Scripture by a faithful use of responsible historical and grammatical scholarship. We affirm that the original meaning of the text is to be given its due primacy. Further we believe in the unity and harmony of its various books and two Testaments so that

one place of Scripture may not be expounded so as to be repugnant to another. Also, it is only by referring to the whole Canon of Scripture that Scripture will be allowed to interpret Scripture. We hold to the sufficiency and trustworthiness of Scripture in bringing unbelievers to Christ and nurturing and sustaining believers unto eternal life. By following these principles of interpretation the Church will interpret Scripture in accord with its nature as the Word of God written.

Is it too much of a stretch to view Judaism in the same way as this document asks us to view the Old Testament—as one of the parts of our holy text? No Christian would remain silent if the only passages read in public worship had to be from the Old Testament. For us, the Old Testament is framed and completed by the New. Nonetheless, we are not surprised when a minister takes his or her text from the Old Testament. We know that the sermon will almost certainly reflect a conversation between the Testaments and that the resulting lesson will be thoroughly Christian. If in that sermon the minister quotes a rabbinical commentary on the text, we will likely compliment him. Wouldn't it also make sense if the minister had a Jewish friend with whom he discussed the passage and from whom he had gained a Jewish perspective? Would any Christian—conservative, fundamentalist, or liberal—object to this kind of interaction? Not likely. Our appreciation for the Old Testament should extend to the descendants of those who wrote and preserved it. Nothing is harmed by asking those people—the Jews—to discuss the Scripture with us.

Besides, isn't the New Testament a Jewish document? Wasn't St. Paul giving a perspective on the emptiness of mitzvoth performed without conscious intention—without faith, in other words? In doing this, was he not merely repeating the charge of the Hebrew prophets? Didn't Jesus begin His ministry with a sermon in a synagogue about the words of Isaiah? Doesn't the New Testament offer Jews a perspective about what was going on in the part of their family that they disowned and disinherited? How then can we disentangle ourselves from one another?

What would it be like to ask Jews to read the New Testament with us and to honestly tell us what they see there?

Many years ago, we asked a highly respected rabbi in our city to give the morning message at our church. To our surprise, he read from the Sermon on the Mount. Rabbi Faulk taught us a few things that day about the style of preaching and the ways of interpreting Scripture used by first-century

Jews. (His doctoral dissertation was about first-century Judaism.) The rabbi repeatedly asked our permission to continue as he dealt with our holy text. From time to time, he stopped to apologize if he were inadvertently saying anything that gave offense. In this way, he continued to gain our support as he shared the words of Jesus with us. As a result, our knowledge of our own Scriptures was deepened, our relationship with the rabbi warmed, and our tense connection with Judaism relaxed.

Like all Christians, I long for the day when our ancient divisions with Judaism come to an end. Through the centuries, though, this very longing has motivated some Christians to bring Jews into conformity to Christianity by force. It has happened from the other side as well. The hostility only pushes us further away from one another.

Many secular Jews railed against Mel Gibson's right to film and promote *The Passion of the Christ*. They tried to use power to suppress our ancient differences. Christians resented this and pushed back by renting thousands of theaters, making Gibson's movie a box-office hit.

The reaction of Jewish producers did not help us heal. Jews would have had a better reception had they organized discussion groups between Jews and Christians, perhaps a few weeks after the raw emotion from the movie had subsided.

Jews need to discover the evangelicals who are often anxious for a relationship with them. This is a new opening for Jews into the heart of global Christianity. They need to realize that the same people who went to see *The Passion of the Christ* are usually open for a dialogue with Jews. Although in some cases these new discussion partners lack theological sophistication, many are willing to learn, and they desire to become real friends. As more Jewish leaders become aware of this new spiritual reality, they may realize that there are more profitable connections to be made with Christians than the ones they have attempted to make with the old mainline Protestant groups.

In short, Judaism remains our schoolmaster, our older brother whose approval we crave. At the same time, the stumbling block remains—the simple carpenter who is David's Son but who claimed to be David's Lord. Christians see Him as the Torah who became flesh and dwelt among us. We believe He is the king of Israel who granted citizenship in the house of Jacob to all those who are weary and heavy-laden. But how can we hope that our estranged elder Hebrew brother will ever believe these things until we acknowledge his continual role in our family? How can Judah hear us until we demonstrate in word and deed our profound grief for all the ways we have abused the caretakers of the covenants and promises?

As we learn in the book of 1 Maccabees, the light from the lamp in the besieged temple at Jerusalem did not go out. The ancient Greeks could not extinguish the flame even when the oil was exhausted. That is why, on December 24, in the year 164 BC, the Jews rededicated the temple to the glory of God. That is why there is a season called Hanukkah.

It is no coincidence that every December 25, Christians celebrate Christmas. When Early Christians forgot why they were lighting candles at the end of December, they gradually came to associate the celebration of Hanukkah with the birth of Christ.

So it is, at the darkest time of the year in the northern hemisphere, the candles of both Testaments burn bright, lighting the way in a darkened world for the seekers of truth to make their way to the house of God.

The candles illuminate the world together: two Testaments to the glory and love of our Creator, who became a Jew in order to invite us all to become the sons of Abraham.

Every time I approach the altar to remember my Lord's final Passover meal, I see two candlesticks, one on the right and one on the left. As I eat the bread and drink from the cup, I am supposed to remember that I am a child of two covenants. Sometimes I look at the candlestick on my left and say a prayer of gratitude for the ancient people who were the first to hear and obey the voice that spoke from heaven. I remember that I was grafted into an ancient vine and that God has promised us that the vine will one day be whole again and that its fruit will fill the earth.

For the mouth of the Lord has spoken it.

the way of the cross:
christianity and global relativism

We preach Christ crucified, to the Jews a stumbling block and to the Greeks foolishness, but to those who are called, both Jews and Greeks, Christ the power of God and the wisdom of God.

1 CORINTHIANS 1:23-24

Father Victor Liakovich commanded the attention of the room long before he began to speak. Even while Glen was introducing him, most of the eyes in the room had been turning to look at the middle-aged priest making his way to the front. We were hardly listening as Glen told us that Father Victor was a priest in St. Michael's Ukrainian Catholic Church, near downtown Pittsburgh. We were too busy watching a man who looked as though he had stepped right out of the fertile imagination of Dostoyevsky or Tolstoy and into the material world of the Franciscan retreat center.

Father Victor had a beard that covered most of his massive upper chest. A large silver chain hung below his beard, and on it was a cross of the Eastern type, with a small horizontal bar above the longer one and another smaller diagonal one below. I remembered that the top piece represents the placard the Romans placed above Christ's head: "Jesus, King of the Jews." The bottom piece represents the footrest that supported Christ's nail-pierced feet. Painted on the cross was Jesus, with a look of joyful suffering on his face. At the feet of Christ was a skull, meant to be that of Adam, the father of humanity, about to be redeemed by the dying man above him.

As he prepared to speak, Father Victor shuffled his papers on the stand. He had a look of intensity. At first glance, I thought he seemed stern, perhaps even angry. Then, when he began to speak, his voice was so deep and textured, he seemed to be about to break into song. I sensed a gentleness that contrasted with his size and sense of authority.

I won't bore you with a long history lesson about my particular branch of Christianity. However, by way of introduction, I am a priest of the Ukrainian Catholic Church. We believe that our spiritual family began when St. Andrew preached the gospel of Jesus in what is now Kiev. A beautiful church stands on the very spot where he is said to have preached. I have been there, and I have a painting of it in my church office.

The more historically verifiable part of our story began in the year AD 988, when Vladimir the Great, king of Rus, was baptized and healed of blindness. He adopted Christianity as the official religion of his people. Because the roots of our nation grew from Constantinople rather than from Rome, our church has followed the Eastern rather than the Western form of Christian worship. So, fortunately for my wife and children, our priests can marry. Also, we worship more like Eastern Orthodox than like most Roman Catholics.

In 1596, the Ukrainian church established full canonical ties with Rome in what is called the Union of Brest. We are, then, along with several other Eastern-rite, non-Roman Christian communities, in full communion with and under the authority of the bishop of Rome—that is to say, the pope.

Living out our faith as we do, at the crossroads between Eastern and Western Christianity, creates a certain amount of friction. We sometimes feel as though we belong to neither community. At other times it feels as though we belong to both.

Many of the books I have back on my table are from St. Vladimir's Seminary Press—an outlet for Orthodox publications. A couple of them were written by the late Father Alexander Schmemann, an Orthodox priest whom many people—including me—consider a saint. (I once audited a class he taught, and what I learned there deeply influenced me.)

Anyway—if you want to know more about Eastern-rite Catholic churches, I will be glad to answer any question I can between our sessions. Before moving on though, I will say that in my opinion, Eastern-rite Christians are often better equipped, both by culture and by theological inclination, to understand non-Western religions than Western Christians. (I trust I do not offend my Roman Catholic or Protestant friends in saying this.)

In the Christian West, theologians have often been lawyers or linguistic experts. For this reason, Western theology, whether Roman or Protestant, often tends to take on a judicial tone, more concerned with definitions and minutia than with spiritual awareness—or so it seems to us in the Eastern tradition. Theologians from the East, on the other hand, tend to be artists and mystics. For them theology is not so much a science built on inferences from Scripture as it is a quest for God in mystery and spiritual longing. Although we are in submission to the authority of the Holy Scripture and to Christian tradition, for us a theologian is more a man who prays than a man who ponders.

For all these reasons, I am moved by the things I have heard here from many of you. When I hear you speak about meditation, chanting, and other manifestations of your piety and spiritual life, I can relate. In fact, when I meditate, I often recite what we call "the Jesus prayer": "Lord Jesus Christ, Son of God, have mercy on me, a sinner."

So, like many of you, I meditate, though what I call meditation probably differs from the meaning you give the word. There is a wonderful little Russian book about how Eastern Christians meditate called *The Way of a Pilgrim*. Perhaps some of you from other traditions would find that book interesting. (I actually have a few copies with me.)

Well, what exactly is Christianity, at least from the standpoint of an Eastern-rite Catholic? Simply put, Christianity is the living presence of Jesus Christ experienced through the lives of those who believe him, especially as they gather together in His name. Christianity is Christ Himself, offered through His church, for the life of the world. Christ is God who became a man, founded a church, and now woos all people to Himself through His church. Christians are those who respond to His call.

Christianity Is Exclusive

The difficult thing to say in a meeting like this is that Christianity is not an inclusive religion. I don't mean by this that we cannot be friends—even very good friends—with those whose views we do not embrace. Christians can embrace any and all people; we cannot however, embrace any or all ideas.

Put another way, people are equal in the sight of God; ideas are not.

I trust I will not come across as too abrupt or unkind for saying this; I realize that exclusivity is not a notion that postmodern intellectuals accept easily. However, orthodox Christians cannot believe that all the beliefs and practices represented here are equally true. At least one cannot do this and remain faithful to Christianity as it has been defined through the centuries. I realize that many Western churches in this country have been redefining what it means to be Christian. Whether this indicates spiritual progress or apostasy is another matter.

Why do I say this?

Well, I came here to learn from all of you. If possible, I want to make some new friends. However, one does not become a true friend through falsehood or through identity theft. One can only become a real friend by presenting his real self. That is my intention. I am a Christian. Therefore, I should tell you what it means to be a Christian.

As I have listened to all of you tell about your faith, I have been trusting that you are telling me what you really believe. I do not know what it means to be a Taoist or a Hindu. Furthermore, I cannot know what it means to live these religions if you hide from me the things about your faith that you fear might be offensive or jarring. Though we may seem to be respectful to one another when we fail to share our real beliefs, we actually show more respect to one another when we "take the gloves off." That allows for real intimacy and interaction.

The fact is, our religions are very different one from the other. Moreover, our differences are profound and fundamental. Otherwise, history would have been much different.

Of course, as has been said here several times, we share many beliefs about justice, morality, and so forth. Christians have always recognized this. Early Christian thinkers, whom we call the church fathers, taught a doctrine called "common grace." It meant that all human beings have access to certain notions about God and morality. As Jesus said, "Your Father in heaven…sends rain on the just and on the unjust."[1] St. Paul also speaks about this in the first chapter of his letter to the Romans. He says that every human being in every culture has known how to live simply by contemplating nature. Therefore, in areas such as morality, science, and law, Christians make no claim to privileged information. We can learn much from one another about such things.

I can also learn from what the various traditions teach about the inner life of the mind. Our knowledge about the mind derives from observations made by intelligent people over many hundreds or even thousands of years. Since we share a common human nature, these observations are often extremely valuable for all of us. They do not have to come from our own Scriptures.

We share even more beliefs with the other two Abrahamic religions. For example, at every mass, we hear readings from the Hebrew Scriptures, which we share with the Jewish people. When we celebrate the sacred meal that Christians call the Eucharist, or Holy Communion, we use words and symbols borrowed and adapted from the Jewish Passover.

Acknowledging the things we share with Islam is a bit more complicated and often causes controversy on both sides. However, Christians obviously share many spiritual practices and beliefs (and certainly much history) with Muslims as well.

I must acknowledge that sharing beliefs and practices with the other Abrahamic faiths has not made our relationships easier. The pogroms against Jews in Europe (not to mention the horrifying holocaust of more recent memory) weigh upon our hearts. For many Christians and Jews alike, these tragic sins have shaken their confidence in God and in the very idea of religious life. The Crusades are another example of our troubled relationships with other religions. In that case, Christians could not live peacefully with their Muslim neighbors. Therefore, we must conclude, spiritual similarities and even theological common ground does not always make us more capable of living together in peace. Sometimes, familiarity really does breed contempt—or much worse.

For a Christian, the basis of living in peace with others must be the belief that we are all made in God's image and likeness. Our Creator do not excuse any of us for harming any of the rest of us, even if we do that harm in His name—no, especially if we harm one another in His name!

For all these reasons, my genuine respect for you requires me to state in what ways we differ as well as the ways we agree.

Let me move on to those areas that I believe express the real essence of Christian faith.

Christianity Teaches That the Universe Is Real

I will not spend much time talking about our worldview. Our Jewish speaker, Dr. Aaronson, did an outstanding job doing that. I have little to add to her presentation of that topic. In short, like Jews, Christians believe that the universe is a creation. A willful and intelligent Creator made our world for His own purpose and according to His own plan.

Therefore, the universe is not eternal. Neither is it an illusion. The universe is not a part of God. The world and all it contains, including us, have been granted an independent existence, though creation is perpetually dependent upon the graciousness of its Creator. He eternally sustains all He has created. We are therefore a dependent life form. We are not, however, an extension of God. We are persons.

These are among the basic ideas of our worldview.

We share this worldview with Jews and Muslims. We do not share the worldview of secular materialists, animists, monists, or polytheists. We serve a personal Creator who wishes to relate to us as persons. As Dr. Aaronson said, this separates us at fundamental levels from many other religions and philosophies.

Christianity Revolves Around the Cross

People often assert that the essential doctrine of Christianity is the incarnation—the belief that God became a man. However, as we have heard here, Hindus believe that both Rama and Krishna were incarnations of deities. So I think Christianity differs principally with all other religions in the manner in which we believe God chose to reveal His love to the world.

Christ, begotten of God before all worlds, died on a cross. That's the way God chose to show that He loved us. The crucifixion was the ultimate demonstration of vulnerability, the deliberate self-abasement of the Almighty. Angry men nailed God's hands and feet to a piece of wood. This means that God deliberately became helpless, as if He meant to say, "Please come closer; I will not harm you."

For us, then, the cross has become the cosmological tipping point, the fulcrum of history. It is God's chosen metaphor both to illustrate and to incarnate His view of reality, creation, sin, and redemption. The cross forms the foundation for Christian doctrine and piety. Thus, the eventual end of human suffering, although yet future, was initiated and made possible by the cross.

The ultimate effect of Christ's work on the cross will be all-pervasive and will redeem every clod of dirt and every blade of grass. The grace of that future event sustains us even now when we walk through trial and suffering. For this reason, Christians experience joy in the midst of their suffering; no, even more—they experience joy *because* they participate in (rather than withdraw from) unavoidable suffering. Christ showed us how to do this on the cross.

Believers are privileged to join Christ in what the New Testament calls "the fellowship of His sufferings."[2] We are not masochists; Christians should avoid suffering if possible. However, sometimes suffering cannot be avoided. And sometimes suffering should not be avoided because avoiding it would leave some redemptive work undone.

This was the dilemma of Jesus Christ the day before His crucifixion. He probably could have left Jerusalem and saved His life. Remaining in the city would mean His death. In the garden of Gethsemane, He wrestled with this knowledge that doing what He had come into the world to do would cost Him His life. In some ways, His emotional anguish in the garden was as great as what He would face on the cross itself. He even prayed that night for another way to redeem humankind.

Like us, Christ did not want to suffer. He chose to suffer not because suffering is in itself good but because in His case, suffering was the unavoidable way to a higher good. At times, this will be the case in all of our lives. That is when we decide to accept or to reject Christ's invitation into "the fellowship of His sufferings."

When I was at the University of Pittsburg, I joined a Protestant group for a while called Campus Crusade for Christ. At the time I had been disillusioned with my Catholic upbringing, so I was reading a lot of Zen Buddhist literature. Frank Spellman, one of our campus chaplains, loaned me a book by a Protestant writer named Tucker Callaway called *Zen Way—Jesus Way*. I was immediately intrigued by Callaway's vivid metaphors of the Zen experience. As I continued reading, Callaway began to demonstrate the utter incompatibility of Zen with Christianity. He did it in a way that showed great respect for Zen, but he did it nonetheless.

Callaway convinced me that trying to downplay the differences between Buddhism and Christianity was disrespectful to both religions.

It was Callaway's ideas about suffering, however, that became the turning point in my own spiritual journey. I actually went to confession the day after I finished reading his book. Then, after confession, I went to mass for the first time in four years.

In essence, Callaway said in his book that Christians do not have the option of treating suffering as unreal. For us suffering is an unavoidable feature of a fallen world. To be sure, Christ came to redeem His creation from its fallen condition and to make all things new. His works impact and transform our suffering, but suffering nonetheless remains real because the fallen world, which causes our suffering, is real.

The full impact of this understanding about how suffering is redemptive came clear to me as I reflected on how Callaway contrasted the symbol of Buddhism with that of Christianity.

The Buddhist symbol is the lotus flower. It remains detached and unspotted by the filth and decay in which it grows. The junk around it never mars its pristine beauty. So, a Buddhist will tell us, the practice of detachment allows a practitioner to walk through life without allowing the illusions and sufferings of this world to stick to him. In fact, Buddhist practitioners learn that they don't even have a self to which corruption can stick!

The symbol of Christianity, on the other hand, is the cross, an instrument of unbelievable cruelty. The cross is stained with the blood of an innocent victim. Therefore, the cross stands for our unavoidable and total involvement in the human condition.

The world actually exists. Individuals exist too, which means that our suffering is not an illusion. Suffering is the reasonable response to a fallen world. However, the cross reminds us that the Creator did not remain aloof from our suffering; indeed, He deliberately plunged into it. He asks His followers to do the same; to take up our own cross and to follow Him as He serves the people of a fallen world.

For the Christian, then, the cross is beautiful because it is ugly! The cross tells us that God is an alchemist! He brings light out of our darkness. He brings joy out of our tears. He does not keep His distance from our pain but rather joins us in our pain, and that makes pain redemptive.

Our belief in the redemptive death and resurrection of Jesus Christ upon a cross implies that authentic spiritual life requires the voluntary embrace of suffering when it comes our way. This separates orthodox Christianity not only from other world religions but even from those versions of Christianity that sidestep the cross. Therefore, Christians must struggle to keep the cross at the center of things, especially in an age in which endless fun is thought to be our inalienable right.

We struggle to value redemptive suffering even within our own community. In the end, the greatest challenge to our faith actually does not come from other world religions; it comes from the secularized forms of our own faith. Just because people continue to congregate as believers and sing joyful songs does not mean that they share the worldview of Holy Scripture or of the saints.

Jesus once said, "I am the way, the truth, and the life; no one comes to the Father except through me."[3] This forces us to make a decision: Either Christ was right about this, He was wrong about this, or He was well-intentioned but trapped by the understanding of His own times. At any rate, if He was wrong about being the way to God, He cannot be the Son of God. In that case, Christianity is seriously (and irreparably) flawed. However, if He truly is the way, the truth, and the life, He is that for all peoples in all times and in all places. Furthermore, because Christ chose to redeem us on a cross, that is where we must meet Him. To avoid the cross is thus to avoid Christ, and to avoid Christ is to avoid God.

Christianity Is a Community

Our faith also informs us that Christ founded a community through which He would continue His work of redemption. This institution is called the church. It is the conduit through which God gives grace and guides His people. To do this, God uses consecrated objects, consecrated time, consecrated people, and consecrated actions. The theological term for these vehicles of God's presence—the sacraments—is "means of grace."

The exact number of official sacraments differs according to the various Christian traditions. Some Protestants even hesitate to use the word "sacrament" at all. However, most churches recognize the following actions as having spiritual significance. In *baptism,* one dies to the world and is resurrected into new life. The *Eucharist,* or Holy Communion, is where we celebrate our restored relationship with God. *Ordination* is the way we safeguard the authority and doctrine of the apostles to our present day. In *holy matrimony,* we consecrate the love between a man and a woman, making covenant between them and God for the purposes of growing them in Christ, propagating the human race, and extending the Christian faith into the future.

The Christian church thus stands with one foot in time and one foot in eternity, serving a fallen world as the body of Christ. It gathered the Holy Scriptures, defined the nature of God and Christ, guided the faithful through the rise and fall of nations, and continues to advance the kingdom of God through service, through the proclamation of the gospel, and by embodying the presence of the risen Lord in corporate worship.

Christianity Is About Service to Others

Jesus voluntarily laid down His life for others and instructed His followers to do the same. Even the leaders of the church are instructed to serve before they govern. For this reason, no man can be ordained a priest who has not served first as a deacon. Deacons are to the church what nurses are to the hospital. They stay close to the nasty realities of life. Deacons sweep. Deacons run errands. Deacons serve. If a man refuses the work of a deacon, he cannot become a priest or a bishop. Furthermore, he remains a deacon forever, whatever else he becomes. Even a pope is a deacon as well as a prince.

I understand that the reality does not always match the theory! History is full of examples of church leaders who were despotic egomaniacs. Church leaders are, alas, also fallen creatures. Now and then, though, some Christian leader emerges who is not only great but also good and who leads through service.

Christian leaders must serve because they must be examples of the Christian gospel in deed as well as in word. We must lay down our lives on behalf of others. We must be willing to die but never to kill. Individually and corporately, Christians must extend Christ's redemption out into the world. They must do this by proclaiming, and they must do it through serving.

This nation is full of examples of how the Christian ethic of service works. Every city in America has hospitals, the YMCA, the Red Cross, the Salvation Army, the St. Vincent de Paul Society, food kitchens, and homeless shelters provided by Christians for the benefit of humanity. Mr. Burtrano last night claimed that these institutions are incapable of sustaining society because they aim only at individuals. Well, I only ask you to imagine what this country would be like without all these entities I have mentioned and the thousands more I have not. Besides, nations come and go—individuals live forever. Therefore, individuals are infinitely more important than nations.

All over the world, people know that if no other place will take them, they can always find help in those buildings marked with a cross. Under the cross, people can always find food, shelter, and a cup of cold water given in the name of the crucified Lord.

So, "we preach Christ crucified, to the Jews a stumbling block and to the Greeks foolishness, but to those who are called…Christ the power of God and the wisdom of God."[4]

JOURNAL NOTES

Father Victor is a real masterpiece! I am thoroughly convinced that he is a servant of God and a brother in Christ. So affirming most of the things he said today about our faith is easy for me. Still, he and I represent groups with historical differences, and I must address them.

As he was speaking, I wrote down a few of the ways in which Protestants differ from Roman Catholics and Eastern Orthodox Christians. Our old differences with these groups are far from settled after all, and we must either justify them or abandon them. Otherwise, we have no legitimate reason for remaining separate.

As Father Victor talked, I thought about the season of my life when I had explored as honestly as I could the differences between Protestants, Catholics, and Orthodox. During that time, my Orthodox friends were certain that I was about to convert. I became intense about learning and discussing the ideas of the church fathers, the Eastern theologians, and the historical saints. In the end, though, I remained a Protestant. However, now I was not a Protestant simply because I was not a Roman Catholic. I was a Protestant because I was convinced of the tragic necessity of the Reformation and of the biblical justification for its central beliefs.

I gradually became aware of the importance of the great doctrines of the Reformation:

> Solo Christi,
> Solo gracia,
> Solo fide, and
> Solo Scriptura.

The Latin phrases mean "Christ alone," "grace alone," "faith alone," and "Scripture alone." In other words, Christ is the only means of grace, grace is the unmerited favor of God, faith is the only required human response to grace, and Scripture is the ultimate authority in theological and spiritual matters.

The Reformation

The Reformation was not, as Protestants have often depicted it, a one-sided fight of righteous men against wicked papal tyrants. It was rather a complicated reaction of northern Europe against Rome. It involved political, economic, social, and technological factors as well as spiritual ones. Furthermore, the Protestants were not always (or even usually) united. Lutherans

the way of the cross

and Calvinists never really came together. The aims of the Anabaptists differed profoundly from those of the Anglican church. Nationality was nearly as important as doctrine to most Protestants.

As soon as Rome had been challenged, the differences between the challengers erupted. Some Protestants wanted to reform the church; others wanted to dismantle it and began anew. Some wanted bishops as leaders, others wanted a council of presbyters, and yet others wanted to dispense clerical leadership altogether and replace it with the democratic rule of the congregation.

The factors of the Reformation are therefore too complicated to even mention here except in the most superficial way. Henry VIII wanted a new wife and used the growing Protestant influence in England as an excuse to ignore the pope. The Anabaptists wanted democracy. Calvin wanted a theocracy. Luther wanted freedom from his personal anxieties about sin, sex, and damnation. Zwingli wanted to evangelize the world. The English bishops wanted enough social stability to lead their churches peacefully through a gradual reform.

These were hardly uniform or even compatible goals. Nor did the Protestants always act from pure spiritual motivations. Nonetheless, the Reformation, messy as all human movements are, provoked massive spiritual change. Western Christians, whether within or without the Roman church, would be forever altered by its fervor, its intellectual challenge, and its spiritual vitality.

The Protestant challenge was above all things directed at the church itself. Was the church so divine that it was incapable of error and human failing? The Roman church seemed to say that it was. The Protestants disagreed. Luther shocked the world by declaring that bishops are merely men, and therefore holy convocations of bishops are subject to error. The pope is, he said, the bishop of Rome, and so we should respect that office. The pope is not, however, the vicar of Christ or the head of the church. Therefore, pronouncements of a pope, while important and worthy of study, are human opinions. They must be examined by ordinary believers in the light of Holy Scripture like any other sermon by any other man.

Soon such opinions were racing across Europe, thanks to the newly invented printing presses. The masses gathered to hear theological papers written in their own languages and entered into the debates that were reshaping their continent. St. Paul was once again upsetting religion and causing chaos! In the midst of the confusion, believers rediscovered the Bible and restructured their governments.

The Reformation fell into a thousand spiritual traps. Protestants quickly grabbed for the centers of power that they had only recently denounced. They used and misused their new power to advance their cause and to punish dissent. They afflicted Jews and burned heretics; they destroyed art and pillaged ancient monasteries. However, slowly the ideas of the Reformation educated the people, restored human dignity, promoted human freedom of expression, and captured the soul of Europe for generations.

Centuries have come and gone since the Reformation. Today, many of its institutions have become massive monuments to a great past. Huge portions of historical Protestantism became a slave to European culture and followed the continent's thinkers in a gradual abandonment of faith. Sociologists and cultural critics have been observing this apparent reality for decades now. But the guardians of culture did not feel the earth move when masses of alienated people from beyond the country clubs and the ivy-covered walls of the great seminaries began to grasp for meaning and significance in the faith Europe had largely abandoned.

There are many streams of neo-Protestant Christianity. Each one has a story to tell, and each one has something to contribute to the surprising resurgence of Christianity around the world.

A half-blind African-American named William J. Seymour represents one part of the story of Protestantism's resurgence among America's underclass and among the peoples of the third world. He was a simple man with a burning heart. Born in slavery, he found his freedom not only through his nation's Proclamation of Emancipation but also in the red letters of his King James Bible. As he preached and prayed, thousands came to his little church in Los Angeles to begin the greatest global advance of Christianity since New Testament times.

Philip Jenkins tells the story more eloquently and more carefully than I can. In *The Next Christendom,* Jenkins reveals that Christianity's core has shifted from northern Europe and North America to South America, Africa, and China. Jenkins bewildered Christian leaders in our country on both the left and the right by describing the massive advance of Christianity in the southern hemisphere. As liberation theology and other half-baked attempts to control and exploit the masses of the third world floundered and failed, a real revolution occurred that few in our country seemed to have noticed until entire nations had become deeply influenced by evangelical faith. A new wave of Christian thought and community had been forming from Colombia to Calcutta and from Buenos Aires to Beijing.

Is it Protestantism? Yes, but often of a terribly uninformed and woefully inconsistent sort. Its power is in its ability to adapt. Its creative impulse grows from its firsthand experience with the suffering and longing of the world's peoples. The folks on the bottom of our technologically interconnected and our economically mechanized world hunger for the presence of God. They have been longing to participate in the blessings of creation and civilization. They have found in Christ Jesus a liberator as well as a Savior and have responded to Him "with exceedingly great joy."[5]

The weaknesses of the emerging global church include its lack of biblical knowledge, its tendency to equate ignorance with piety, its thoughtless acceptance of the worst features of American popular religion, and its lack of connection with Christian history and theology.

My belief that these are dangerous faults is a minority opinion. It often gets rebuked. My words, however, are not those of an enemy. Furthermore, I have earned the right to speak, having been deeply involved in the spread of the gospel in many countries, usually among the poorest of the poor. Furthermore, the church of the southern hemisphere taught me the ways of God. I am its child. I celebrate its growing leadership over the churches of God throughout the world. Nonetheless, it is vulnerable and does not yet demonstrate the ability to grow roots that will sustain coming generations.

The emerging Pentecostalized churches in the global south could learn much from the likes of Father Victor. Even when we disagree with him, he forces us to explain why. He makes us define who we are and what we believe. Moreover, whether we like it or not, Father Victor represents our history, the good and the bad, without which we will lack the necessary foundation to pastor and disciple the masses we have won.

The churches of the global south need not only to discover their ancient roots but also to understand Protestantism. The crucial doctrines of the Reformation—the centrality of the cross and the priesthood of believers, for example—are in great danger in the third world churches and in newer churches even in our country. The anti-intellectual mood of much of the southern hemisphere exposes the church to dangers that a healthy resurgence of Protestantism could address.

Protestantism's error was that it failed to include the human emotions in worship and devotion. It became rational to the point of absurdity. It focused on the head and neglected the heart. It taught that our emotions had fallen in Adam but seemed to act as if our intellect had not. The emerging global church often reacts against this history by going in the opposite direction. It acts as if our emotions have not fallen and thus cannot deceive our minds. It focuses on miracles of deliverance but neglects the need for an intellectual grounding in the faith.

Father Victor's central theme, that the cross is the core of our faith, must be heard. This message does not sell. It does not market well. It does not bring the masses to their feet or move them to shout for joy. However, it remains the center of the gospel, which is "the power of God to salvation."[6]

A few months before I wrote these words, two young leaders in our church died in a car wreck. They were on their way to a missions conference. As our shocked congregation prepared for their funeral, I stood outside preparing to process the tragedy, trying to collect my wits for the homily. I was lifted out of my despair when I heard a thousand young voices loudly singing of Christ's victory over sin and death.

The young voices reminded me that the human part of our faith—our individual and corporate reactions to God's grace—can be messy things. However, the risen Christ, whose name we bear, guides us through the mess and always fulfills His promise never to leave us.

Like the mess of the Reformation, the faults of the church in the global south will result in unavoidable harm. People will sin. Leaders will commit fraud. Cults and sectarianism will arise. However, if history is any guide, we will also witness economic, social, and spiritual growth in many nations long resistant to the gospel of Jesus. Whether this will be followed by another radical reaction against superstition and anti-intellectual piety, however, depends on the wisdom and courage of Christian leaders. They must wrestle with their responsibilities to cultivate culture and mind as well as to comfort soul and heart. Christianity is, after all, not a thing we see, but rather something through which we see everything else.

11

a guide for the perplexed:
finding our way in a globalized world

When all around my soul gives way,
He then is all my hope and stay.

I left the Franciscan retreat center on Friday evening at about six. The joint worship service would begin at 7:00, and I had decided not to attend the service. But I did want to eat one more meal with some of the folks I had met during the three-day conference.

We had all loosened up since Wednesday, so our conversation around the table was lively and congenial. I sat with Mariana Alvarez, the worship leader of Asamblea Cristiana del Redentor in Yuma; Father Ramsey Hartford-Smith, rector of All Saints Episcopal Church in Las Vegas; Victoria Williamson from the Center for Global Consciousness in Payson; and Dr. David Choi of the Korean Presbyterian Church in Los Angeles.

Mariana began talking almost immediately about Father Victor. She remarked that she had been shocked to hear a Catholic priest talk about his wife and children and then go on to say that he had once belonged to Campus Crusade for Christ. Ramsey gave her a short history lesson about the Uniate Eastern churches. Victoria said that the Ukrainian priest made her think of Father Zossima in *The Brothers Karamazov*.

The other two Americans laughed when I started humming the theme from *Doctor Zhivago*. When Mariana asked me to explain what the song was about, I started to explain but then quickly decided that an explanation required too many layers of generational background. Dr. Choi politely smiled at the entire exchange, but he never said what he was smiling about.

We went on to discuss the current split within the Anglican churches and how this may be the beginning of a schism that will ultimately affect Christians everywhere. Dr. Choi remarked that Presbyterians are facing the same issues as Anglicans and that their division is along similar lines: Westerners on one side and the rest of the world on the other. Ramsey then added that the division was particularly painful because people like him had always thought of themselves as more sympathetic to the churches in the third world than were the more conservative types.

Mariana kept trying to understand why the American Protestants seemed so confused. She wondered why didn't they just read their Bibles and learn what God thought about the issues. Dr. Choi then explained that many American Protestants no longer read the Bible the same way she does, which seemed to leave her more confused than ever.

Victoria said that she figured that some Christians in America were "rising above spiritual provincialism to embrace a more universal perspective." She added, "This is inevitable really, though it must be painful for those who are not ready to make the journey."

Mariana seemed to take the conversation in an entirely new direction when she told the story about how she had once been addicted to cocaine. She had walked the streets of San Diego as a homeless woman for a while, she said. She went on to say that she had met a street preacher from Tijuana who attended a church that met at a bull-fighting stadium. His words had been so impressive that she had knelt in the street to pray. After living several months in a halfway house, she had moved to Mexicali to attend a three-year Bible school program. After graduating, she had accepted an invitation from a small church in Yuma that met at the Holiday Inn, and she had been there since.

Our conversation seemed to lose its energy after her story. When we finished our coffee and sherbet, we each dismissed ourselves from the table, promising to stay in touch.

I walked toward the parking lot, knowing that my world had somehow changed in the three days I had been at the conference. For a long time, I would not be able to put into words what I had experienced. But I already knew that the reality of the new century had somehow broken through to me as I had listened to the various speakers.

For the past several years, I had been trying frantically to lead our church the way I had been taught. I had kept insisting to myself that our nation was still basically the same as it had always been. Any day now, Andy Griffith would walk back into our lives and restore civic decency. Soon Christian young people would grow up, and then they would understand that the music we had used in church 40 years ago was still the best way to praise God. The illegal immigrants would all return home. Telephone operators with thick accents would not answer from half a world away. All these cultural changes around us were merely fads; good Christian leaders just needed to stay the course.

As it turns out, the world's cultures are boiling over. Things will never return to the way they were before the Internet, before the end of the cold war, and before the planes plunged into the World Trade Center. Americans would never again be able to isolate themselves from the rest of the globe. What happens today in Hong Kong will affect the economy tomorrow in Hot Springs. A new cult that begins this week in Istanbul may spread to Indianapolis before the year is out. Our borders are broken and easy to breach. No politician and no preacher will ever be able to give us back our old world.

So I had a decision to make. Either I would fume and fuss, alienate and divide, or I would learn how to reflect the gospel of Christ in a dangerous and confused world. Choosing to be a Christian instead of an angry old man would require me to realize that I had a lot to learn about the world's peoples. It would also require me to make some real friends with folks who thought and behaved very differently than I did.

It all boiled down to whether I wanted to become effective or merely comfortable.

Effectiveness could not mean neutrality or spiritual relativism. I am a Christian. I believe the words that St. John wrote so long ago: "God did not send His son into the world to condemn the world, but that the world through Him might be saved."[1]

Not only am I a Christian, I am an orthodox Christian, trying to confess that which has at all times and in all places been believed by the whole people of God. Like St. Paul, I want to be able to say, "I am not ashamed of the gospel of Christ, for it is the power of God to salvation."[2]

Nonetheless, the peoples of the earth, now brought together in closer relationship than at any time since Babel, must learn how to listen to one another. We cannot hope to win the world to Christ through war, economic conquest, or any other form of hostile engagement. Were we to achieve any sort of victory over the world's peoples through aggression, the religion established by such means could hardly be the faith we are committed to spread. We are limited then to the methods of our faith as much as to its doctrines. We either convince the world's peoples through love, truth, and service, or we cannot convince them at all.

In our times, perhaps more than at any other, we must learn to listen as well as speak. We have no right to expect to be heard if we do not have enough humility of heart to listen.

How can I tell a Muslim that Jesus died on a cross if I refuse to listen to him tell me that Muhammad introduced Moses to a quarter of the globe?

Can I expect a Buddhist to hear me say that Jesus saves if I refuse to acknowledge that the Buddha was a very great teacher?

Can I witness to a Native American without a sense of profound repentance for the bloodshed and for the fictitious history that has been perpetrated against Native peoples by professing Christians?

Listening wins the right to speak. Serving wins the right to relate. Loving wins the opportunity to share. This is the heart of things: The gospel in word and action is simply sharing Jesus with the world's peoples.

Many Christians in Western nations are perplexed. We are not leading the global church anymore, and that feels strange. The cloud has moved. However, we still have work to do here in our part of the world. Many of us would like to do it in the ways we have always done it. However, we are hitting a wall because the old ways seem not to work anymore. So we tend to separate into crazy dichotomies like "liberal" and "conservative." But those labels only relieve us of the burden of thinking for ourselves. They allow us to drift into a complacent denial of our faith or into a boring and angry orthodoxy. That's not a very appealing choice for our children or for the unbelievers.

Christians in the global south seem to be preaching the gospel. They seem to be expecting God to show up in power to transform their lives and communities. All over the world, believers have been erasing old boundaries between Christian groups and borrowing from one another whatever they need to proclaim Christ. To me, that is a much more appealing model than trying to market Jesus to skeptical people. I have often wondered, why can't we study like Presbyterians, save souls like Baptists, honor Communion like Anglicans, pray for the sick like charismatics, build schools like Methodists, and dance like African-American Pentecostals? What holds us back except sectarian pride? Maybe the world will start taking us seriously when we start taking one another seriously!

So I'll conclude this book with a few suggestions about how I think we can reach people in our globalized, post-Christian, postmodern world.

Christians Should Embrace Their Own Faith

It seems easy now for a Christian to write a book for other Christians that ridicules and mocks our own traditions. It seems easy to assert that Christianity is not a religion at all and then to add, "good riddance" to nineteen hundred years of art, prayer, theology, and architecture as though all of our history were some evil encrustation—"barnacles on the hull of the old ship of Zion," as one preacher put it.

I disagree.

The gospel is neither advanced nor hindered by the cultural artifacts that its people have created through the centuries. The artifacts are merely material witnesses to our ancestors' appreciation for the gospel.

A real seeker is neither attracted nor repulsed by our customs and traditions. A seeker merely wants to know where God is. The artifacts of our faith—stained glass, great hymns, ritual protocol, and the like—may tell the seeker about where God has been. Certainly, if God is no longer there—if He is not peering through the things our ancestors created to announce His presence—the seeker has the right to be upset. In that case, our artifacts become a form of false advertising.

On the other hand, if we remove all symbolic representation of God's presence in order to woo one who is seeking God, we lack integrity. We become like a man who invites a new acquaintance to his house to meet his wife. However, first he decides to remove any pictures, letters, or personal articles that belong to her.

What would we think of a host who would ignore his wife or try to keep her in a back room while his new friend is visiting? We would not be convinced were he to tell us that he fears his wife's presence might spook his guest, that he must therefore introduce her gradually, lest her presence startle and upset his new friend.

This, I suggest, is the spiritual condition of many of our American churches. They have been deliberately eliminating any possibility that the presence of the God they wish to introduce to the world will intrude upon the consciousness of those who visit His house. That is not meant to be harsh; I believe that churches that have been secularizing their worship have done so in order to reach out to unbelievers. However, I believe this path is false and is becoming spiritually damaging.

I believe we have done this because American Christians tend to confuse worship and evangelism. Worship is awe. It is a believer's visit with God and eternity so he or she can focus on things of ultimate value. Evangelism is the work of introducing people to God. Using this definition, worship is not the proper place to do evangelism.

We rarely meet new friends in our homes; we usually meet them in hotel lobbies or in restaurants—in neutral places, in other words. The walls of such neutral places naturally do not contain symbols of our family life. Nevertheless, once we make acquaintances, we usually invite those acquaintances into our homes, at least if they are interested in forming a deeper friendship with us.

That, I would offer, is how one relates to a seeker. Once he or she becomes an acquaintance, we should not be afraid to share our family life.

A person offering a relationship with another does not spring into existence immediately before the relationship is formed. People with whom we are building relationships have histories. They come from others who have histories. All this history has gone into creating their personalities, their thoughts, and their tastes.

Christians also have a history. They should not pretend that they are secular people or that they are disconnected from Christian history. When they offer relationship to others, they offer all that made them what they are.

On the other hand, the Bible does not prohibit Christians from experimenting with styles of music, technology, or organizational models. Surely we can honor the past without worshipping it!

A Commitment to the Study of Scripture

An increasing connection with other religions necessitates that we become more informed about our own. Otherwise, fear forces us to either remain aloof from others or to compromise the uniqueness of Christ out of a desire to relate. When we know our own faith well, we cease being afraid of others. However, we cannot know our own faith well without studying the Holy Scriptures.

Using our Bible as a talisman, like some sort of magic, does not help us or others. We need to know the history, context, and genre of literature of the various parts of Scripture. We need to understand how to do proper exegesis. My son-in-law, who teaches and promotes a Bible training program called Veritas, continually emphasizes this to me and to anyone else who will listen.

We also need to know how to use the Bible devotionally. When the Bible becomes a part of our daily journey of prayer and meditation, we gradually learn how to live a different kind of life. Slowly, our lives become compelling reflections of God's glory. We become what St. Paul called living epistles, "known and read by all."[3]

We need to know the Bible because unbelievers need to know more about the Bible. A real seeker who wants to study Islam will not resent reading the Koran. A real seeker learning about Judaism will not run away from the study of Torah. Real seekers are looking for authenticity, not for "bait and switch." So although we must present the stories and studies of Scripture in compelling ways and may use contemporary sources to illustrate the points, our attention must be upon the Scripture itself. The Word of God opens the heart to the presence of God. It instructs the mind with the thoughts of God. It motivates us to do the work of God.

An Appreciation for Our History

Church history is not a peripheral subject for any believer. History shows what happens when the gospel is proclaimed and when cultures react to that proclamation. History tells what kinds of things can go right and what can go wrong in God's name. When we know our history, we learn what to do and what to avoid. We find things to admire and things for which we must repent. Christians have blessed the world with hospitals, colleges, orphanages, publishing houses, churches, and mission stations. Christians have also caused sorrow and distress in the Crusades; the enslavement of Africans; the violent conquest and subjugation of the Incas, Aztecs, and other Native cultures; and the centuries-old harassment of the Jews. For all these crimes we stand accused before the world and before our God. Knowing these things brings humility of heart and encourages a commitment to serve God and humanity in our own times with grace.

In the end, Jesus remains compelling in spite of the historical atrocities we have committed in His name. The peoples of the world still love Him. So the world continues to offer us opportunities to preach Christ in word, in deed, and through our own transformed lives. We will not be able to stay on track, however, if we forget both the good and the evil of our own history.

An Understanding of Our Contemporary Culture

We must understand our times. This is not America of the 1950s, and it will never be that again. If we define Christianity in a way that is not based in contemporary reality, we will create communities of socially isolated people, increasingly disconnected with those Christ came to save.

So we must address contemporary questions. We cannot afford to slice and dice the gospel in ways that make it the plaything of our social and political preferences. Science must be heard and respected. We must listen to those who care about the environment. Health care issues are serious for Christians as well as non-Christians. Addictions afflict believers as well as nonbelievers and so must be addressed.

We may not agree with the way others respond to these questions of our time, but we cannot ignore the questions. Neither can we disdain or ignore the people who ask them. The questions provide a meeting place where we can share Christ and serve humanity in His name.

Understanding our contemporary culture allows us to speak the language of the people who live around us. Although we are in many ways countercultural, we must learn to connect where we can and in ways that are winsome and kind whenever possible. That's what Jesus did; that's what we must do.

Conclusion

I wrote this book from the premise that a seeker wants to know God and wants to meet others who know God. Therefore, a seeker expects to meet God with and through those who claim to follow Him. This means that God should not be sold and marketed; He should be genuinely manifested.

When people decide that God may exist, they become hungry to meet Him. At this point, people will not care about the cultural context in which God shows up. If people really believe that God will be there, they will go to any sort of church and listen to any kind of music. The cultural package becomes a peripheral issue at best when one really becomes a seeker after God.

But people are seeking for God and not merely a connection with people who claim to follow Him.

A man may enjoy a good play about Santa Claus. He may form friendships with those who perform a play about Santa Claus. However, his life will not be changed drastically by these new friendships. But consider what would happen if he were to witness a man riding a sleigh through the sky pulled by reindeer! He would soon be doing a lot more than making friends with actors; he would be altering his view of reality! That is what conversion is—changing one's fundamental views about what is real and about what is the purpose and meaning of life. Therefore we need the supernatural presence of God to stand behind the words we proclaim.

Spiritual seekers ask cosmic questions like that. They want to know what is real. Is there infinite intelligence behind our universe? Is my short life of any real consequence? What happens after I die? Do nonmaterial intelligent beings exist? Do sane people ever meet these beings?

Increasingly, making a claim to believe in God, angels, and life after death, but not living as though these facts really alter one's practical day-to-day life, looks like dishonest escapism. For this reason, defining a seeker as someone who wants to make friends with nice people—folks who have the good sense to not mention the supernatural—seems fundamentally dishonest. This approach to Christianity draws people who are not profoundly interested in ultimate things. It draws people who are looking for a consciously contrived fantasy around which to form relationships—rather like Star Trek groupies. It repels the real seekers, the sort who say, "Sir, we wish to see Jesus."[4]

To call a person a seeker then is to imply that he is searching for something. So we must not only define seekers, we must determine what the seekers are seeking. One can search for fine cuisine, for a way to reconcile general relativity theory with particle mechanics, for a love-crazed turkey on the first day of hunting season, or for toothpaste at Target. Seekers after God want God; they are not primarily after a better light show or gourmet coffee. If a church builds its infrastructure around offering better coffee, it will attract those who want better coffee. Newcomers may accept the coffee and gather at the church that offers it. They will not necessarily meet God, however, because that was not what was being offered.

As the years have passed, I have sometimes grown sad about church life in America. Our numbers have grown, but the presence of God has often diminished, or so it seems to me. Our paint is fresher, our organization is tighter, our marketing is spectacular, our salaries are better. All of this effectiveness seems to draw people. It certainly helps us form good, healthy community. Meanwhile, I think about a young Hindu woman who was not asking me how to cope, but about who was Jesus and about what He wanted with her.

I don't think the Hindu woman was asking for an intellectual answer, as important as that is. She certainly wasn't asking if we had comfortable seating at our church. She was asking if Jesus was in our church and if she could possibly meet Him there.

It is deeply offensive to most of us to realize that many of the most serious seekers in our culture have been passing us by. They are unmoved by our lattes and our rock bands. They have concluded that the resurrected Christ, whose cross we have removed in order to make the seekers comfortable, is not present in many of the churches that confess Him.

Many of these seekers have been moving into the other religions of the world, where they are offered a new way of life, an experience of presence and an up-front declaration of otherness that separates them from the culture of secularism. We need to understand why this is happening. We must allow it to shock us into a fresh encounter with the presence of God, offered through the Word made flesh, the study of Holy Scripture, and the sacramental grace of the gathered people of covenant.

In looking at other religions and at other forms of our own faith, may we too become seekers, even if our search moves us to abandon all the modern parodies of religion in order to find Him who made us for Himself and for whom our hearts incessantly yearn.

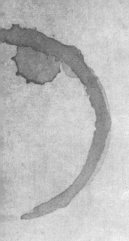

a discussion
guide

I added this section of the book mainly to facilitate group discussions. However, it will also help those who may wish to go deeper in their own private reflections about what they have read here regarding the religions of the world. The best way to use this section is to read each of the questions and then allow conversation (or private thought) to emerge in response. In a group setting, the questions may evoke passionate responses. That is the nature of religious questions. The most productive groups will be those in which the participants are allowed to address not only about the various responses to the questions, but about the emotions surrounding the responses. Each response can thus promote learning, especially when the participants are asked to support their responses. Sometimes, a story from one's own spiritual history can be particularly valuable in promoting community and thus in making group participation an exciting and rewarding experience. Because this book offers such brief descriptions of the great world religions, discussion and reflection about the book's content may help a reader gain a much deeper knowledge of the beliefs and practices of those religions.

Introduction: What Is a Seeker?

1. What do Christians usually mean by the word "seeker"?

2. People of other religions usually have sacred texts of their own. So, what becomes the connection point between a Christian and a person who follows another faith?

3. What does the author mean by the "secular" trance that he claims has "mesmerized" much of evangelical Christianity in the United States? Do you agree with him?

4. What does one say about the secular orientation of most North Americans, including North American believers, and the spiritual/sacred orientation of many people in other parts of the world?

5. How would you define Christian orthodoxy? What is the difference between essential matters of doctrine and practice and the cultural forms through which those essential things are expressed? Give some examples of different expressions of Christian faith that each manifest orthodox Christianity in different ways.

6. Why do you suppose the author refused to participate in a worship service with representatives of other religions but agreed to participate in an exchange of opinions?

7. Do most Christians need at least a superficial knowledge of the great world religions? Why or why not?

8. Other than your own faith, did you discover that you had more sympathy for one of the other religions than for the others? What do you think this reveals about you and your spiritual walk?

Chapter 1—Oh My, Other People Are Out There!

1. Discuss how your nation and the world have changed in your lifetime. How has technology changed the experience of borders and boundaries between nations, peoples, languages, and religions?

2. How have the various generations of Americans experienced these changes? How have their different perspectives altered the ways in which each generation practices its faith?

3. What do you think about Philip Jenkins's claim that worldwide Christianity is dividing between North and South, much as it did in 1054 between East and West? What are the implications? Does your church (or do you personally) relate most to the churches north or south of the equator?

4. Why do Jenkins and Scott claim that "liberalism" and "conservatism" often mean different things in the global church than they do to believers in North America?

5. What does Amos Yong mean when he talks about the Holy Spirit being at work in places where Christ is not yet named? Is the Holy Spirit ever at work among people of other religions? Why or why not?

6. What can we learn from Abraham's encounter with Melchizedek in our work with people of other religions? From St. Paul's experience on Mars Hill?

Chapter 2—The Great Harmony:
Taoism and the Chinese Worldview

1. Has anyone in your group ever read the Tao Te Ching? Could someone bring a copy and read a few pages?

2. How would you characterize the approach to life that these passages from the Tao Te Ching suggest?

> The Way that can be expressed is not true;
> The world that can be constructed is not true.
> The Way manifests all that happens and may happen;
> The world represents all that exists and may exist.
>
> To experience without intention is to sense the world;
> To experience with intention is to anticipate the world.
> These two experiences are indistinguishable;
> Their construction differs but their effect is the same.
>
> Beyond the gate of experience flows the Way,
> Which is greater and more subtle than the world.[1]

3. Discuss the aspects of the Chinese experience that Redman claims are contrary to Chinese philosophy. Speculate about how these characteristics impact the manner in which a Chinese person might experience God, faith, and revelation:

   • A common civilization stretching back through time,

   • a common written language, that the Chinese, regardless of their particular dialect, understand,

   • and a common worldview that unites the Chinese, regardless of their religious affiliation.

4. What impact did Confucius have on China? What do you know about him?

5. What impact did the Buddha have on China? How did China impact Buddhism?

6. What is known about Lao Tse? How did his work impact China?

7. What do you think about the way James Redman compares modern American attitudes toward old and traditional things with the attitudes of many Chinese toward tradition?

8. How do you feel about how traditional Chinese culture is presently impacting American culture in such things as these?

   - acupuncture
   - Chinese medicine
   - fung shui

9. How does the worldview behind the practice of the I Ching differ from the worldview held by most Western people? Does the Bible say anything about worldview? Think about ways that divination was used in the Bible; comment on how these might have worked in the lives of believers.

10. What would you say about the questioner's comment that James Redman had been duplicitous about presenting Taoism in a more secular and less mysterious light than its history seems to warrant? What about Redman's retort that people could judge many modern presentations of Christianity in the same way?

Chapter 3—The Rivers All Flow into One Ocean:
The Allure of Hinduism

1. Do discoveries made in physics (such as the theory of relativity and quantum mechanics) have theological implications? Is this even an important question? Why or why not?

2. Is postmodernism really a "kind of cultural despair; a sense of Western defeat for having been wrong about profound things?"

3. What are some implications of the belief that the universe is conscious and that all parts of the universe share in that consciousness?

4. What does Dr. Upadhyaya mean when he says that it is equally true to say that Hindus believe in many gods, that they believe in one God, and that they believe in no God?

5. If anyone in your group has seen *The Thirteenth Floor,* ask him or her to summarize the experience of watching the movie. How does it express the worldview of Hinduism?

6. Would Christians from the second century really feel bewildered by modern Christians' view of the supernatural? What, if any, are the implications?

7. Why can't Christians view matter as unreal or at least as a lesser realm of identity?

8. Do you agree that Christians should not join Hindus in worship? Why or why not?

9. What things about Hinduism do you find intriguing? Disturbing?

10. Why do you believe some scientists find Hindu philosophy intriguing?

Chapter 4—The End of Suffering:
Following the Buddha in the Surrender of Self

1. Why did Torri Adams begin her talk by singing "Row, Row, Row Your Boat"?

2. Why might she have chosen the joke she did?

3. Discuss Adams' description of her struggle with racial identity and how she uses it to claim that all peoples' perceptions of themselves are similarly constructed.

4. Discuss the Four Noble Truths:

   - Life is difficult (or suffering).
   - Suffering is caused by craving.
   - Nirvana, or the end of suffering, occurs when we stop craving.
   - Nirvana can be reached by following the eight-fold path.

5. How does the movie *Groundhog Day* illustrate Buddhism?

6. How do the modern theories of physics open the door to Buddhist philosophy?

7. Is Buddhism better categorized as philosophy, psychology, or religion?

8. Discuss the implications of the Three Jewels:

- I take refuge in the Buddha.
- I take refuge in the dharma (teachings).
- I take refuge in the sanga (community).

9. What are the similarities between Christianity and Buddhism? Differences?

10. The author says that "we need more than a teacher; we need a Savior." Why does he say this? What is the difference?

11. Buddhists believe that self is an illusion. Christians believe that we are called to be persons through our relationship with God. What are the implications of these very different views of self?

12. Why are many American intellectuals so sympathetic with Buddhism?

Chapter 5—At One with the Earth:
The Native American Way

1. Francisco Puma claims that the "rape of Native America was, like slavery, perpetuated by a Christian people who claimed to stand on high moral ground." What should a Christian say to this?

2. Discuss the meaning and practice of shamanism.

3. To what does the term "Native medicine" refer, according to Puma? Did you follow his thoughts about the connections between the English words "whole," "holy," and "healthy"?

4. What does Puma mean when he says movement is life and that healing thus involves a restoration of movement? What part does drumming and dancing play in Native America?

5. Do you agree with the author that "Western TV shows...demeaned and humiliated the peoples whose land we systematically pillaged"? Why or why not?

6. The author says, "from a Christian standpoint, Native American religion includes several wrong answers about fundamental questions." Do you agree or disagree?

7. Are we really "not inclined these days to recall the dark side of Native American life"?

8. Do you agree that those "who worship nature become poor and unlearned"?

9. How important is it to say "God is not nature, and nature is not God"?

10. What should a Christian's view of the environment be? How does the concept of stewardship differ from that of veneration?

Chapter 6—The Spiritual Smorgasbord: New Age and a New American Culture

1. How does the so-called New Age movement reflect long-held American tendencies?

2. How did European philosophy lay the groundwork for the New Age movement?

3. Discuss the differences between objectivity and subjectivity. Is objectivity possible?

4. Why does Walter Summers refer to Teilhard de Chardin? Discuss de Chardin's ideas as presented by Summers.

5. What about Summer's view of his neighbor? Is the neighbor simply afraid of the modern world, as Summers claims?

6. Discuss Summers' claim that the New Age movement views gods, demons, and other spiritual entities as archetypes, as symbols of psychological realities rather than actual beings. What about his references to Thor?

7. What does the following statement mean, and what does it imply about the New Age movement?

   I have no orthodoxy to protect and no confession to satisfy. I merely experience as much of this brief life as I can. Whatever seems helpful, I use. Whatever seems unhelpful, I avoid. I don't try to explain or judge spirituality; I merely experience it.

8. Is the New Age movement a religion? Why or why not?

9. Why does Harold Bloom claim that gnosticism is America's default spirituality?

10. What do people mean when they claim to want spirituality but not religion?

11. Do you agree that much of American Christianity is heavily influenced by the same spiritual concerns as those within the New Age movement?

12. What is "civil religion"? How does it compare to historical Christianity?

a discussion guide

13. Do you agree that many spiritual seekers do not view the various kinds of Christianity as viable options for them? Why or why not?

14. Discuss the story of Archbishop Tay's visit to Vancouver and the subsequent split in the global Anglican Communion.

15. Why is the concept of evil important, and why is it mentioned in this chapter on the New Age movement?

Chapter 7—Submission to Allah: The Way of Islam

1. How did you react to Nurbekov's conversion story?

2. Were you surprised that Islam, Christianity, and Judaism share common roots?

3. Discuss Nurbekov's definition of jihad as "moral exertion." Do Christians believe in this? Why or why not?

4. How does the Islamic view of the Koran compare with a Christian view of the Bible?

5. Discuss Muhammad's role as a cultural architect—the founder of a new political and cultural society.

6. How does Islamic reaction against globalization compare with the reaction of other traditional religious communities?

7. What contrast does the author highlight between Islam and the teaching of St. Paul?

8. Is submission the first principle of spiritual life? Why or why not?

9. Why does the author claim that the canon of Scripture was closed after the acceptance of the New Testament? Discuss the process of canonization and why nearly all Christians believe that process to be closed.

10. Should religions become states? Should religious leaders seek to become political leaders? Should political leaders seek to make their religious beliefs into law that unbelievers must obey? Why or why not?

11. How does the Islamic view of monotheism compare and contrast with that of Christianity? How do these different views impact a view of community, dissension, and difference?

12. Why is Islam making converts in the United States?

Chapter 8—Sole Judge of Truth:
The Path of Secular Humanism

1. Batrano claims that "civilization's oldest connecting cords—the religious ones—are gone forever." Is this true? Why or why not?

2. Discuss Batrano's observation that Christianity has reacted to secularism in three different ways:

   • by accommodating the faith to culture,

   • by limiting the faith's concerns to matters of piety, and

   • by a hostile entrenchment in the thought forms of the nineteenth century.

3. Do Christians really ignore the structural causes of human suffering even when they focus on individual needs?

4. What do you think of Butrano's assertion that religion is art more than science? What does he mean that religion is drama?

5. Are all of the world's religions, including Christianity, really becoming steadily more secular in their beliefs and practices?

6. Is humanism really a religion? Why or why not?

7. Why do you believe that American academia ignored Solzhenitsyn? Why did he condemn both Western democracies and Soviet culture?

8. Discuss these three terms:

- Christian liberalism
- Christian fundamentalism
- Christian orthodoxy

9. Are secular cultures really less violent than religious ones?

10. What does the author mean when he claims that humanism is dead? Is he right? Why or why not?

Chapter 9—The People of Covenant: Judaism and the Way of the Book

1. In what ways is the Torah a schoolmaster?

2. Discuss the various kinds of Judaism described by Dr. Aaronson.

3. What makes the word "Jew" so jarring to so many people?

4. Why do you think Jews tend to do so well in so many fields?

5. Discuss the story about the rabbi in the concentration camp who claimed to lose his faith in God but who nonetheless kept his appointment for prayer.

6. What does Aaronson mean that God calls His people out of the cultures where He encounters them?

7. What role do the Sabbath and Passover play in preserving Judaism?

8. What is a mitzvah, according to Aaronson?

9. Why do you think Christian attitudes toward Jews have swung between such extremes throughout the centuries?

10. Why does the author say that modern Judaism is no more (and no less) a legitimate descendent of ancient Hebrew faith than Christianity? Do you agree? Why or why not?

11. What issues influenced the break between Judaism and Christianity? Will the break ever be healed? How?

12. Discuss the Anglican Mission in America's statement on the relationship between the Old and New Testaments. Do you agree with it? What are the implications of this statement?

13. Can Jews and Christians worship together? How? Can they discuss Scripture and spirituality in mutually beneficial ways?

Chapter 10—The Way of the Cross:
Christianity and Global Relativism

1. How does Father Victor claim that Eastern Orthodox theologians differ from Western ones? Do you agree?

2. Why does Father Victor claim that Christianity is an exclusive faith?

3. Do you agree with Father Victor that authentic dialogue between religions should focus on difference as well as agreement?

4. Why does Father Victor say that the cross is the center of Christian doctrine? Is he right? Does a loss of emphasis on the cross really undermine the Christian faith?

5. Discuss the contrast between the Buddhist symbol—the lotus—and Christianity's symbol—the cross.

6. Do you agree that the church is the institution through which God brings Christ to the world? What is the church?

7. How important are the sacraments in the life of a Christian? What is a sacrament?

8. Was the Reformation really a "tragic necessity?" Why was it tragic? Why was it necessary? Was there another way?

9. What are the implications of Philip Jenkins' claim that the center of Christianity has shifted to the nations south of the equator?

10. What can historical churches learn from the emerging churches of the global south?

11. What can the emerging churches of the global south learn from the historical churches?

Chapter 11—A Guide for the Perplexed: Finding Our Way in a Globalized World

1. How would you define a spiritual seeker?

2. Why does interaction with other religions require a deeper knowledge of one's own faith?

3. How do we deepen our understanding of our own Scriptures? Of our own history?

4. Why and how should we gain a better understanding of our own culture? How do we critique culture in the light of Scripture?

5. How do scientific discoveries impact our view of Scripture? Is there a right or wrong way to compare and contrast contemporary discoveries and Holy Scriptures?

6. Why does the author claim that many contemporary approaches to Christianity abandon the discussion of ultimate things?

7. What can we learn from the great world religions? What can we share with the followers of other religions? How do we go about sharing with them?

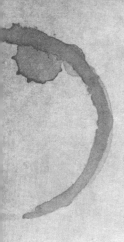

notes

Chapter 1—Oh My, Other People Are Out There!

1. Amos Yong's writings include *Hospitality and the Other* (Maryknoll: Orbis Books, 2008), *The Spirit Poured Out on All Flesh* (Grand Rapids: Baker Academic, 2005), and "The Future of Asian Pentecostal Theology," *Asian Journal of Pentecostal Studies,* vol. 10, no. 1 (2007).
2. See Acts 10:28.

Chapter 2—The Great Harmony: Taoism and the Chinese Worldview

1. Romans 1:21 KJV.

Chapter 3—The Rivers All Flow into One Ocean: The Allure of Hinduism

Epigraph. Rig Veda, 1:164.46. Quoted in Linda Johnson, *The Complete Idiot's Guide to Hinduism* (New York: Alpha Books, 2002), 52.
1. Adapted from Johnson, *The Complete Idiot's Guide to Hinduism,* 146-47.
2. Stephen Mitchell, trans., *Bhagavad Gita: A New Translation* (New York: Harmony Books, 2000), 49.
3. Hebrews 13:2 KJV.
4. 1 John 3:2.
5. Philippians 2:7 NASB and NKJV.
6. Ephesians 2:7 NASB.
7. Hebrews 2:4.
8. Ephesians 2:1.
9. John 1:14.

Chapter 4—The End of Suffering: Following the Buddha in the Surrender of Self

Epigraph. From the Dhammapada (Sayings of the Buddha), quoted in Lama Surya Das, *Awakening the Buddha Within* (New York: Broadway Books, 1997), 130.
1. Philippians 4:8.

2. Romans 12:2.
3. From Charles Wesley, "Jesus, Lover of My Soul," published in 1740.
4. From Henry L. Gilmore and John Sweney, "The Haven of Rest," published in 1890.
5. Psalm 119:7-8.
6. John 6:68.
7. 1 Timothy 3:15.
8. Psalm 100:3.
9. Romans 3:23.

Chapter 5—At One with the Earth:
The Native American Way

    Epigraph. Quoted in Vine Deloria, *God Is Red* (Golden, CO: Fulcrum, 2003), 146.
1. Psalm 8:5; Genesis 1:27.
2. Ephesians 6:12.
3. From John Keene, "How Firm a Foundation," published in 1787.
4. 1 Kings 8:27; 2 Chronicles 2:6; 6:18.

Chapter 6—The Spiritual Smorgasbord:
New Age and a New American Culture

    Epigraph. Marianne Williamson, Illuminata: *A Return to Prayer* (New York: Berkely Publishing Group, 1995), 53.
1. Helen Schucman and William Thetford, *A Course in Miracles,* vol. 3 (Mill Valley, CA: Foundation for Inner Peace, 1992), 429.
2. Colossians 2:18.
3. Ephesians 3:10.
4. Harold Bloom, *The American Religion: The Emergence of the Post-Christian Nation* (New York: Simon & Schuster, 1992).
5. Judges 17:6; 21:25.
6. Jude 3.
7. See Philip Jenkins, "The Next Christianity," *The Atlantic Monthly,* October, 2002.
8. Exodus 20:3-4.
9. Galatians 1:8.
10. From Martin Luther, "A Mighty Fortress Is Our God," 1529.

Chapter 7—Submission to Allah:
The Way of Islam

1. Koran 96:1-5.
2. Galatians 5:1.
3. Romans 5:8.
4. Matthew 11:28.

Chapter 8—Sole Judge of Truth:
The Path of Secular Humanism

1. From the fifth-century Vincentian Canon.
2. Romans 3:23.

Chapter 9—The People of Covenant:
Judaism and the Way of the Book

1. Galatians 3:24 (KJV).
2. Abraham Joshua Heschel, *I Asked for Wonder,* ed. Samuel H. Dresner (New York: Crossroad, 2002), 35.

3. Heschel, *I Asked for Wonder*, 87.
4. Ephesians 2:14,19.
5. Galatians 3:7,9,28.
6. Romans 9:4.
7. See, for example, Isaiah 37:32.
8. See Isaiah 6:13.
9. Acts 7.
10. Acts 15:14-19.
11. From the Book of Common Prayer.

Chapter 10—The Way of the Cross: Christianity and Global Relativism

1. Matthew 5:45.
2. Philippians 3:10.
3. John 14:6.
4. 1 Corinthians 1:23-24.
5. The phrase is used of the Magi in Matthew 2:10.
6. Romans 1:16.

Chapter 11—A Guide for the Perplexed: Finding Our Way in a Globalized World

Epigraph. From Edward Mote, "On Christ the Solid Rock I Stand," published in 1836.
1. John 3:17.
2. Romans 1:16.
3. 1 Corinthians 3:2.
4. John 12:21.

A Discussion Guide

1. From GNL Tao Te Ching, interpolated by Peter A. Merel. Available online at www.chinapage.com/gnl.html.

It's a Harsh,

Crazy,

Beautiful,

Messed Up,

Breathtaking

World...

And People Are Talking About It...

conversant **life**.com

engage your faith